CANNABIS

CULTIVATION & COOKBOOK

A BEGINNER'S GUIDE TO GROWING MEDICAL MARIJUANA & COOKING EDIBLE MEDICAL MARIJUANA

BY JOSEPH BOSNER

TABLE OF CONTENTS

CANNABIS

STEP-BY-STEP GUIDE ON HOW TO GROW MARIJUANA FOR BEGINNERS

BY JOSEPH BOSNER

INTRODUCTION

The human race owes cannabis a sincere apology. Never has been something so beneficial to us treated with so much societal disdain and ascribed a strongly negative stereotype. Never has another living organism offered so many benefits to another living organism in return for thinly disguised apathy. Why do I say this?

Our society a couple of decades ago held strictly negative views about cannabis and its usage. In almost all the countries of the world, it was considered a criminal offense to grow or use cannabis. In most, it was often treated with the same levity as the possession and usage of strict narcotics like heroin and cocaine. Societal prejudice against cannabis even made things worse.

Despite being less harmful and a lot more natural than a lot of other psychoactive agents, it was considered the big, bad monster that should be exterminated from society. Yet, this is the same plant that has existed for thousands and probably even millions of years with us. In fact, available data points to the fact that we met cannabis on this planet.

During these succeeding years, cannabis had proven to be a valuable tool to ancient man and his needs. We soon learned to gather, then, cultivate cannabis for our use. However, the tide changed against cannabis about two to three centuries ago. From being so useful that it was both a drug and a source of clothing material, society began to outlaw its production. Cannabis fall from grace itself was curious, unexplainable and the product of certain economic and social factors.

Today, it stands represented as a drug that can cause social, health and mental problems but is this true? To be honest, cannabis does have its side effects, but these are no way close in severity to what we have been led to believe about this plant. Yes, cannabis may affect motor skills and impair eye to hand coordination as a short-term effect, but then so does alcohol. Yet, nobody has made any move to ban alcohol.

Deciding to drive or operate heavy machinery after cannabis consumption is just as stupid as a decision as driving after drinking alcohol heavily. So, this is really down to a lack of judgment than an exclusive, inherent problem with cannabis use. So many more over the counter medications and drugs can induce this kind of effects too. Do we go around banning them? No!!!

Cannabis is also often represented as being addictive. However, the definitive list of all drugs deemed addictive by psychiatrist, the ICD 10 (classifications of Mental and Behavioral Disorders) seems to have a major omission; cannabis. Surprised? Well, don't be. Cannabis's active ingredient is not nearly as addictive as even the caffeine in your coffee. Instead, deciding to consume cannabis regularly is more of a personal, conscious decision. Therefore, we may have people who may be rightly classified as addicts because of the amount of cannabis they consume willingly, but that is not exactly due to the substance itself. The problem as with many things is man and his propensity to overdo things. The problem is "too much cannabis" and not cannabis. In that regards, this is true for almost every substance we consume.

That is why there is no anti-cannabis drug for chronic users the way heroin or crack users get to take medication. It is simply because there is no addiction. How are the pharmaceutical industries able to sell us some anti-cannabis drugs? Unfortunately for them, they can't because there is nothing to cure with drugs.

Consider this little fact that may have escaped you too. If you have a problem with illicit drugs like opioids, you not only need a psychiatrist, you may also need a GP and even an internal medicine expert. This is because your entire body needs to be evaluated for the damage, they may have caused you. However, that isn't the case with cannabis. If you consume too much cannabis and are trying to reduce the quantity, you get to visit a psychiatrist or psychologist. That is because there is very little if any internal damage caused by cannabis. In any case, a few days of not taking cannabis gets rid of any potential adverse effects it has on the body. The metabolic products may remain a while longer, but the effects disappear once you stop taking it. There are no withdrawal symptoms when you stop the consumption, and your body does not need to detoxify anything simply because cannabis wasn't really toxic to it in the first place.

So, tell me again, why have we exactly criminalized cannabis? Why have we as a race invested billions (in protection and regulation) in trying to limit the growth of a plant that offers so many benefits with a few adverse effects?

The National Household Survey on Drug Abuse estimated that 95 million Americans (age 12 and older) had tried cannabis at least once. Conservative estimates also suggest that roughly 300 million active and consistent users of cannabis abound worldwide. Those numbers would be much more if we didn't call the dog a bad name to hang it.

The bold truth however is that cannabis possession and cultivation still remain suppressed in most places on earth. Thankfully, since the turn of the millennium, better awareness and the realization that we have been wasting money trying to stop what we should encourage has led to a general relaxation of the mitigating laws against cannabis. In most places now, it is quite allowed for you to grow one or two cannabis plants for medical use.

However, because of its suppression over the course of history, information about exactly how to grow cannabis is relatively scarce. This is why I actually wrote this book for you to help with the basics of growing cannabis. Having a general idea of what you will require and the processes involved will better arm you to see your cannabis plant grow to life.

Luckily, cannabis itself is a perseverant plant. It can thrive in almost any clime so long as it receives the right amount of light and an adequately favorable temperature. However, because of the inherent problems involved with cannabis regulation, it is often better to plant your cannabis indoors. This throws up a number of challenges which are what I have tried to help you solve.

With just a bit of skill and determination, the info contained in this book can turn you from willing user to an independent and successful grower. Good luck as you try to bring forth the beneficial and misunderstood plant that is cannabis!!!

CHAPTER 1

WHAT IS CANNABIS?

It is the ultimate herb. Many people regard it as a source of uplift and yet, so many others have also pointed accusatory fingers at. It is cherished yet reviled in turns. It is cannabis, marijuana or any of its various names. In whatever form cannabis is, it continues to be one plant that divides opinions like no other one before it. But what exactly is "cannabis"?

I must introduce you to the plant itself, to that Holy Grass that several have killed and died for. Somehow, we can say it is a secret, an open one jealously guarded especially in recent times by its own users, brave men and women who have defied enormous odds, risking their lives and liberty for pot.

Belonging to the family *Canabaceae*, cannabis is a flowering, annual plant that is also known by other names such as hemp and marijuana. Like us, our plant is of the two genders, male and female and this is why scientists use the loaded term *dioecious* to describe it.

Cannabis - The Plant

A cannabis plant is usually either male or female, although there are some varieties which are both male and female. What this means is that a single cannabis plant can have both male and female flowers growing on it. In fact, the Chinese have long recognized this difference since at least the 3rd Century BC. However, mankind, in its characteristic habit of altering nature for its own gains, has altered the pure strains of Cannabis. The result of this tinkering is plant varieties whose flower types can be both male and female. Yet, they still get called female because they possess more female flowers than male ones.

How does the cannabis plant live on? How does it ensure its own survival? Well, the answer is a simple one: it is wind-pollinated. It has also gotten spread when its pollen gets transported on the bodies of animals especially birds. So, with just one or two plants, a field left to itself can become a bed of cannabis. Another way this plant lives now is our own deliberate cultivation, an art to which this book is devoted.

Can you recognize a cannabis plant when one stares you in the face? No? Well, you must first know that there are other plants which can be confused with cannabis owing to striking similarities. However, knowing what you are looking for simply requires a little training of the eyes; no equipment needed unless you are examining some very tiny samples of the plant. How can you tell cannabis apart? The leaf!

The leaf is the Rosetta stone, the key to telling the difference between the cannabis and the natural charlatans that hold themselves out as the true one. Because the leaves are the most recognizable part of the plant, it is not surprising therefore that they have been the subject of several artworks across the world, from Asia to Africa. While cannabis may be the surname of the plants, it is also indicative of the fact that there are several species or subspecies of it and these are what I refer to as forenames – again, we shall come to them later in this book. The point to note here, however, is that despite the varieties, the leaves are principally similar.

Plant leaves are generally arranged in a simple or compound form and cannabis has a compound one. What this means is that a single cannabis leaf is divided into divisions called leaflets. Ordinarily, a single plant leaf grows from the stem and does not divide. In the case of the hemp plant, the single leaf is divided into opposing pairs and for this, scientists describe it as *decussate*. But this opposing-pair nature does not last long. Once the plant starts to flower, the arrangement of the leaf's changes into an alternating one.

There are two other noticeable features of the leaf: the first is that each leaflet has serrated edges; and the second has to do with the arrangement of the veins on the leaf. A single leaf usually has a total of twelve or thirteen leaflets, with six arranged in opposing pairs and with each pair at right angles to the previous one. Each serration on a leaflet has a vein running down from its tip and another from the point of serration, and the vein from the point of serration usually runs down to form a V shape with the vein that runs to the tip.

Cannabis: The Drug

The word "Cannabis" can also refer to the drug produced from the plant of the same name. This should not form a source of confusion. It's simply like saying 'rubber', a term which can refer to the substance and at the same time the tree from which the substance is extracted. Cannabis the drug is also known as Marijuana. Marijuana is made up of two things: the sticky resin secreted by the flowering tops of the Cannabis plant and the leaves of the same plant. This is what makes it different from Hashish which is only the secreted resin.

Cannabis the drug has been known since 3000 BC in Central Asia, China and the Indian Subcontinent. In fact, in the ancient language of India, Sanskrit, the drug is known as *Ganjika* and in modern languages as Ganja, the same word used for it in Jamaica. The active ingredient of cannabis is known as "delta-9-tetrahydrocannabinol" or simply, THC, and it is one of the 85 cannabinoids derivable from the plant. While THC and *Cannabidiol* (CBD) are the two cannabinoids produced in greatest abundance, only THC is psychoactive i.e. it has the ability to affect moods and behavior.

By now, you can intelligently tell in what sense the word *Cannabis* is used at various parts of this book. On the one hand, the term can refer to the plant and its various species. On the other, it can refer to the drug extracted from the plant. While some parts of this book relate to the plant i.e. it's cultivation and harvesting, other parts deal with the drug itself.

Side Effects of Cannabis

One must not shy away from the truth. If you observe well enough, you will realize that there is hardly anything with loads of merits without at least one or two demerits. Is the usage of cannabis airtight and without any side effect whatsoever? Unless I choose to pretend ignorance, my answer to the question just posed must necessarily be in the negative. Cannabis (the drug) has side effects. In this part of the chapter, I have classified the side effects into two: short term side-effects and long-term side effects.

Short-Term Side-Effects

The short-term effects of cannabis are those ones that are immediately brought about by its use and which do not last long. They are usually experienced for a few hours and then the effects subside. In the following paragraphs, a number of these short-term effects will be discussed with some details.

Cognition and Coordination

Cognition refers to your ability to acquire knowledge. In other words, it is the mental process of acquiring knowledge by the use of perception, reasoning and then intuition. What is the fate of this mental skill when you use cannabis? The answer is that this ability is impaired for a short term, usually a few hours until you get 'low' from the 'high'. Abilities packed together within cognition include: attention, concentration, decision-making, response time, risk-taking, verbal fluency and working memory. All of these cognitive abilities are impaired on a short-term basis by the use of cannabis in certain forms and dosage.

Coordination is a related mental activity and it is equally negatively affected by the use of cannabis on a short-term basis. Coordination here refers to the use of the limbs or other parts of the body in accomplishing tasks such as response to stimuli. A person who is high as a result of cannabis use has their motor coordination equally impaired. A typical example of this is interference with driving skills and the risk of being involved in accidents and other bodily injuries if heavy machinery is used within this period.

Why does this happen? Remember one of the constituents of cannabis is delta-9-tetrahydrocannabinol also known as THC. There are parts of the brain which receive this cannabinoid known as cannabinoid receptors. These parts are also responsible for coordination and cognition and once affected, the above-stated facts are the results.

Increased Cardiovascular Effects

A short-term effect of cannabis use as concerns the heart is a risk of acute myocardial infarction. In simpler terms, it means cannabis users may have a higher risk of a heart attack especially if they have a pre-existing cardiovascular condition. This condition refers to the deadening of the tissue of the wall of the heart usually as a result of the loss of blood flow. Some studies have shown that a cannabis user with a history of myocardial infarction is four times likely to experience the condition in the hour after the use of cannabis. The risk however subsides shortly thereafter and this is why I have classified it as a short-term effect of cannabis use.

Increased Effects on Lungs

The respiratory system is made up of small air passages called bronchioles leading into the lungs. When you smoke tobacco, one of the effects is acute bronchial constriction. This means that there is a constriction of these passages and the blood vessels surrounding them. The opposite is however the case when you smoke cannabis resulting in acute bronchial dilation. Since some people smoke the two, then the effect of on the lungs is inconsistent acute bronchial conditions. Remember, this does not last long and thus it is only a short-term effect.

Anxiety

This is a side-effect more common with first-time users of cannabis. If you are new to the game, you are very likely to experience anxiety, panic attacks, hallucinations and vomiting. This is basically your body system reacting to its very first encounter with cannabis. With repeated use though, these symptoms soon disappear.

Long-term Side-Effects

The discussion in this part of the book covers the long-term effects of using cannabis. A long-term effect can occur even if the user is not a frequent one.

Impairment

Already, impairment has been discussed as a short-term effect of using cannabis. However, there can also be impairment occasioned by using cannabis which lasts longer than the one experienced on a short-term basis. How is this possible? How long does the impairment last? There have been studies carried out to answer these questions and the result is that cannabis use for a long-term has a long-term effect on the user's cognitive skills as well. One of the results was that verbal learning, memory and attention were found to be deficient in regular cannabis user. This is logical since, as pointed out in the short-term effects that cognition is temporarily affected, continued and sustained user means continued effect on cognition.

Another way the use of cannabis can impair cognitive abilities has been demonstrated in another study on the IQ of persons who are constant users of cannabis. The result was that people who were constant users of cannabis experience a substantial drop in their IQ scores compared to people who have never used cannabis and people who used cannabis but were not constant users. However, the results of this study are highly subjective and have not been repeatedly proven.

Cellular Damage

This side-effect relates to the cells in the body of a person. Cannabinoids are fat soluble and can clog the cells to inhibit their functions. Every cell in the body has 46 chromosomes except the sex cells i.e. the sperm and the ova which each has 23 chromosomes. When the two combines, the number comes up to the 46 in the ensuing cell and anew organism begins life. Certain studies have shown that chronic users of cannabis have the highest number of abnormal cells. However, it is still uncertain whether this is due to cannabis use or other lifestyle factors as many of these interlopes.

Organ Damage

THC has also been suspected of causing damage to other organs in the body. Remember, THC is one of the cannabinoids in cannabis and the organs it affects include the brain and the lungs.

The Brain

The brain is the most important part of the human body – it is the most complex organ and biological system in the universe. According to learned opinions, humans have only so far been able to decipher what goes on in less than 10% of the brain. This all-important organ that sits in the skull above the human body can be affected by cannabis use. The complexity of the brain, it must be pointed out, is such that damage to a small part of it can have lasting and far-reaching effects on different things.

First, we know THC alters the hippocampus, the area of the brain responsible for learning and memory and this affects its communication with other parts of the brain. Cannabis use can also alter the development of the white matter in the brain especially during adolescence

The Lungs

Carcinogens are substances that can cause cancer. The rate of cancers in people who use tobacco is 50-70%. Using cannabis though, especially by way of smoking, affects the lungs too. One joint has been said to be the equivalent of five cigarettes. Also, a joint also contains

3-5 times more hydrogen cyanide, nitric oxide and aromatic amines. The results of all of these are respiratory conditions such as reduced lung density, lung cysts and chronic bronchitis, and chronic obstructive pulmonary diseases.

Addiction

While cannabis is said to not contain any chemicals that can get you hooked compared to tobacco and cocaine, it can still lead to addiction. Proof of this is the fact you can yourself identify some addicts around you. So, I will do some more explaining on how you can get hooked on cannabis.

In order to determine when a person has become hooked on cannabis, at least any three of the symptoms discussed next must happen. One, you must have developed a very strong desire or a sense of compulsion to take cannabis. Two, you must find it difficult to control your behavior as far as taking cannabis is concerned with respect to the timing, and the amount you take. Three, your tolerance level for increased dosage must have also increased i.e. you now require to take so much quantity in order to get the usual effect because your body is now tolerating the substance. Usually, such an increased dosage will have very adversely affected a non-tolerant user. Four, you find yourself still desiring and in fact using cannabis after seeing some side effects of it.

Note that the entire process of getting addicted is more mental than biological. That means it is really more of a bad habit as sucking your thumbs than an actual addiction like cigarette addiction.

If you start using cannabis as an adolescent, the risk of addiction is 16%. If you are a constant user, the risk is 30-50%. The problem with getting hooked on cannabis is not just getting hooked; it also means that any side-effects of cannabis use are prolonged. Another side-effect closely related to addiction to cannabis or dependence on it is the likelihood of dying early as a study has shown an increased mortality rate in its use.

Social Problems

There are social problems related to cannabis use. One of these is poor academic performance. Studies have shown that constant users of cannabis usually experience poor grades usually owing to lesser time spent on studies, and poor cognitive skills etc. Equally, a high rate of dropouts has been observed amongst constant users of cannabis.

Given the present restrictions around the sale and use of cannabis in some countries, there is a very high likelihood that constant users of cannabis will also likely abuse stronger narcotics such as heroin and cocaine. This is expected for reasons such as the fact that the cannabis and the other drugs are peddled by the same persons and sometimes commercial cannabis is already mixed with some other drugs.

A final note on the side-effects of cannabis is in order. What has been done here is a humble effort to represent the facts and facts only. Not all side-effects listed in every source have been mentioned for various reasons. Some side-effects have not been properly confirmed so that they are still mere speculations or hypotheses.

In the end, the choice to consume or not consume cannabis is entirely yours. However, quite a large bulk of the medical effects remains unproven. I have only stated them so you know the concerns about cannabis use. Indeed, almost all of the effects mentioned are found only in chronic users who consume a large amount of the drug persistently over time.

Health Benefits of Using Cannabis

In this section of the chapter, the health benefits of cannabis will be discussed. I have spared no efforts in trying as much as possible to record every benefit of the substance known to me. The benefits range from those that are neurological through those that are psychological in nature to those other than these two i.e. miscellaneous ones.

Lessening Tremors in Parkinson's disease

Parkinson disease is a disorder of the nervous system characterized by tremors or trembling of the arms and legs. Muscular rigidity and poor balance are other symptoms of the disease. In some cases, people who have it may not even ascribe these symptoms to the disease because they are usually thought to be the symptoms of old age. The disease also worsens with age. What happens in this disease is that there are a progressive degeneration and loss of function of the neurons that control motor ability in the brain. With this loss, sufferers face a lack of coordination hence the characteristic tremors they experience etc.

Risk factors of the disease include genetic makeup which may make some people more prone to it than others or environmental factors such as heavy industrial activity. There is no cure for the disease. Medications and therapy can however be used to reduce its effects. Recent research has however shown that cannabis, especially when smoked, can reduce pains and tremors associated with the disease. In fact, astonishingly, it also leads to improved motor functions.

Epilepsy Control

It was on one of those summer evenings when he was playing a game of chess with his friends on the porch of his parents' house. He had the upper hand despite playing against two persons at the same time. They could confer but he had just himself. Then all of a sudden, he flipped the board over with a sudden movement of his right hand. Then he lay prone there on the porch, convulsing.

The above is a description of an epileptic seizure. In fact, by the time he recovers, the sufferer will be blank, not knowing what had just happened to him until his own confusion registers to him that he had just blacked out. Epilepsy is one debilitating medical condition that can push victims into the abyss of depression for fear of suffering an episode in public. Studies have shown so far that cannabis can very well help in controlling or even eliminating the risk of seizures. This is achieved as THC binds itself to the brain cells responsible for controlling excitability and regulating relaxation.

Shielding the Brain from Stroke

Stroke is one of the leading causes of mortality and morbidity worldwide. It occurs when there is a shortage of blood supply across the body. Our brain is made up of nerve cells and they require some nutrients to survive. How do they get these nutrients? Through the blood that courses through you. The blood supplies the cells with the needed nutrients and oxygen. Once the flow of blood to the brain is obstructed for a few minutes, the nerve cells starve to death. This may then lead to paralysis (temporary or permanent) or even death in severe cases.

Although I am not aware of any research into how cannabis can be used to combat stroke in humans, that has been demonstrated with lab rats. Cannabis has been shown to reduce the size of the area of the brain affected by stroke and thereby protect the brain from stroke.

Treatment of Glaucoma

Glaucoma is a disease of the human eye caused by increased pressure within the eye. The cause of this disease is simple: the watery fluid within the eye is responsible for maintaining the bulbous shape of the eye as well as supply nutrients to the other parts of the eye such as the cornea. This fluid, called the aqueous humor, has to be drained regularly from the eye. When it is not properly drained and it accumulates, the result is an increase in the pressure within the eye known as the intraocular pressure (IOP). The ultimate end of glaucoma is a loss of vision and when that happens, it is irreversible. Usually, surgery and medication can be used to slow the disease or halt it altogether.

Luckily, according to studies as far back as the 1970s, cannabis has been reported to decrease that pressure, the intraocular pressure, in people with glaucoma. This way, it helps combat the diseases. In those without glaucoma, it can help lower their chances of developing it later on in life.

Relieving Arthritis

Arthritis refers to a range of diseases that cause pain, stiffness and in a majority of the cases, swelling of the joints in the human body. Your body has two types of joints – movable and immovable ones. Your skull has immovable joints known as suture joints. However, your wrist, knees, elbows, neck, ankle, waist etc. have movable joints. As it is normal to for two rubbing parts to experience fiction, the human body has also evolved with this problem in mind and hence, the presence of synovial fluid that provides lubrication at the joints.

Imagine being unable to move your limbs or feeling very great pain moving any joints in your body. Yes, that would be a nightmare and it is still probably, for you, no more than an imagination. Well, pain, stiffness and swelling of the joints in the body is the reality of people who suffer from arthritis but cannabis can help alter this nightmare. Cannabis can help reduce the pain as well as inflammation. It also promotes sleep for such persons, something which the pain can actually deny them. Note, however, that this has only been the case with rheumatoid arthritis, one of the many types there are.

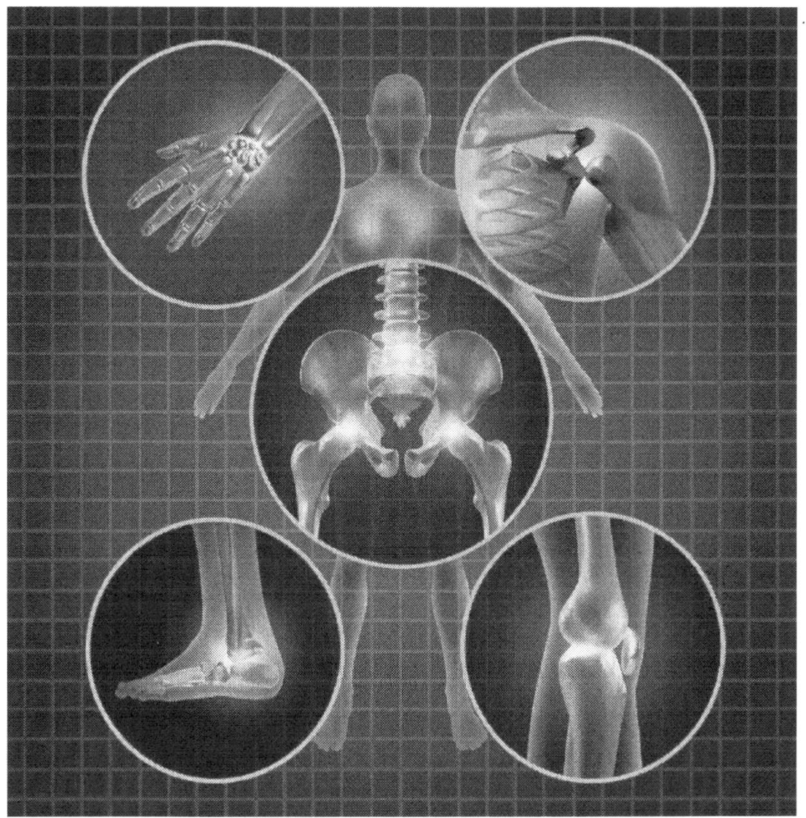

Helping with Treatment of Hepatitis C

Hepatitis is characterized by the inflammation of the liver and this can be caused by virus, bacteria or long-term exposure to alcohol. Basically, when one has hepatitis, your liver is at risk. The liver performs a life-saving function by deactivating the harmful substances that we have ingested into our body. Symptoms of a hepatitis infection include nausea, loss of appetite, jaundice i.e. yellowing of the skin and the eyes that result from the inability of the liver to break down the excess yellow-colored bile in the body.

When hepatitis is caused by a virus, then it can A, B, C or D. Treatment of hepatitis C especially involves therapy and side effects of the treatment include depression, muscle ache, loss of appetite, fatigue etc.

In many cases, people are unable to finish the treatment as these symptoms may last for months. How has cannabis helped?

Well, it has in two ways. According to a study in Europe, 89% of cannabis users were able to complete the treatment – this is significant when compared with 29% in non-users of cannabis. Cannabis also seems to have positive effects in suppressing the replication of viruses in viral hepatitis. Studies show that the viral loads or levels for 54% of cannabis users were relatively low compared to only 8% of non-users.

Slowing Cancer Cells

Cancers occur when the cells in the body multiply uncontrollably until they start destroying healthy tissues in your body. Ordinarily, the human body depends on cell multiplication or division but this has to go at a normal rate – cancer is when this happens at a turbo rate.

CBD is the other very active constituent of cannabis along with THC. In a study, breast cancer was put to the test. Cancer cells make more copy of a gene known as Id-1 and this allows them to spread faster than non-cancerous cells. When these cells were subjected to CBD, a decrease in their Id-1 expression was observed and this impedes their spread. This means that cannabis can have a cytotoxic or killing effect on cancerous cells.

Helping Treat Crohn's Disease

Crohn's disease is one of the inflammatory bowel diseases (IBDs). It is also known as regional enteritis. The cause of the disease is unknown and it affects young adults the most, with people contracting it during their teens. The nature of the disease is a chronic inflammation of the intestine resulting from an extreme reaction of the immune system.

The symptoms of the disease include abdominal pain, diarrhea and weight loss. The lining of the intestine usually becomes inflamed and, in some cases, also swollen creating a kind of cobble-stone effect. In extreme cases, the wall of the intestine becomes pierced allowing digested food and fecal matter to pass into other parts of the body.

In a recent study by scientists, people with the disease were subjected to treatment with drugs containing THC, particularly a 25% concentration. The results were amazing. Complete remission was achieved in 5 out of 10 patients – this means that either the disease was made to disappear or its severity was drastically reduced. Additionally, 10 out of the 11 patients actually responded positively to treatment. Even more astonishingly, there were no significant side-effects of cannabis recorded in these patients.

So far, in this first chapter of the book, the aim has been to introduce you to the world of cannabis. One important thing I am certain you have noted about the word *Cannabis* is the fact it can refer to both the plant and the drug. But, of course, you can always tell the different usages apart. While there may be other plants with a close resemblance to cannabis, you now know what to look for in order to tell cannabis apart from these other plants – you now know the leaf is the key, the Rosetta stone.

Equally, in this chapter, you have been introduced to the harms and benefits of cannabis. You know the pros and cons of its use by now. However, a point I have not stressed about the discussion on the harms and the benefits is the fact you are not to take anything stated in that section of this chapter as medical advice. I have only provided those pieces of information for educational purposes and nothing more.

CHAPTER 2

HISTORY OF CANNABIS (CANNABIS AND HUMAN SOCIETY)

From our previous discussion on its side effects and benefits, one thing is clear – *Cannabis* is a somewhat controversial topic. In this chapter, the aim is to get you more familiar with cannabis. Therefore, the discussion here will center on the origins of cannabis, methods of using cannabis, its usage or purposes for which it is used and the position of the law as far as cannabis cultivation and consumption is concerned.

Origin of Cannabis

It is difficult to recount the history of cannabis with exactitude for the obvious fact that there was a lack of writing system amongst the earliest ancestors of the human race, the very first set of people to consume cannabis. This has therefore made it extremely difficult to say with certainty which group of people first utilized the healing benefits of the cannabis plant and in what form and way they made use of it. Despite this shortcoming, however, we can still attempt some form of reconstruction based on the little evidence we have with us.

Cannabis is believed by experts to have first grown in Central Asia and the upper parts of South Asia, particular in Mongolia and Southern Siberia. It certainly grew on its own before humans intervened to propagate it by deliberate cultivation. As such, cannabis is considered one of the earliest cultivated crops by humans. Its discovery was no doubt by our prehistoric hunter-gatherer ancestors. From what might have been a stroke of luck, cannabis started its life-long relationship with man.

Very likely, its psychoactive nature was probably first discovered by the ancient peoples. If this was really the case, it would have constituted an untapped goldmine of hallucinations. That way, the old folks think it's a gift from the gods or their ancestral spirits, a gift to help create a link between the living and the dead. So, undoubtedly, cannabis would have played a very important role in the development of religious and spiritual thoughts and ideas of human society.

Some centuries ago, cannabis was a source of fiber (hemp) for making clothes and dresses. We are coming to this later. They found it as a good source of rope for tying things. They soaked the plant in their streams and extracted from it interwoven hemp to be used as a rope. From this would later arise the discovery of using the plant for making yarn for clothing materials. All of this particularly fit China's history of clothing choices.

If we try to go back and see how long-ago cannabis has been in use, then you should know that burnt cannabis seeds dating as far back as 3000 BC have been found in the Jurgan Burial Mounds in Siberia. Equally, mummified quantities of cannabis have also been found in burial tombs from Siberia and China, dating back to 2500BC.

The earliest known record of its use for medical purposes dates back to 4000BC when it was used as an anesthetic in surgery. Though according to some other sources, the earliest written record of its use comes from a Chinese document dating back to 2727BC, this claim is debated. There is however, ample evidence to show that the Greeks and the Romans knew the plant very well, too.

Tracing the pattern of invasions, and migrations, cannabis probably left China when coastal farmers brought it to Korea in 200BC. Sometime between 2000BC and 1000BC, cannabis came to South Asia though it had arrived in the Middle East sometimes around 2000BC to 1400BC. It was from there, particularly Sythia (now known as Moldova, Ukraine and Eastern Russia) that it first entered Europe through Russia and Ukraine.

With the Anglo-Saxon invasions, cannabis entered Britain through Germany possibly in the 5th Century AD. The seeds of the plant have been found in Viking ships dating back to the mid-9th Century AD. From the Middle East, it was very likely carried into Africa, particularly North Africa, following the expansion of Islam from the Arabian Peninsula.

The plant probably first entered the South Americas before North America, undoubtedly through Mexico. The plant is now ubiquitous, growing on its own in some areas and being cultivated openly or secretly in others. Cannabis, no doubt, has come to stay.

Usage of Cannabis

In this section of the chapter, the focus will now shift to the purposes for which cannabis is used. In this section, three major usages of cannabis will be focused on. These are medical usage, recreational usage and spiritual usage.

Medical usage

Use of cannabis for medical purposes, I am sure, by now, is no strange idea to you. In fact, the use of cannabis for medical purposes dates back to ancient times. Earlier, I mentioned how the Chinese used cannabis as a form of anesthetics during surgery. There is also an ancient manuscript or pharmacopeia that details the use of cannabis for medical use. There is also evidence of the use of cannabis for medical purposes in ancient Netherlands, Egypt, India and Greece.

Given the contribution of the Islamic world to medicine, then it should come as no surprise that physicians in the Islamic world in the period between the 8th to the 18th century also used cannabis for anesthetic, diuretic, antiemetic, and anti-inflammatory purposes.

In modern times, an Irish physician is credited with having introduced cannabis into the medicine of the western world. Despite the fact that cannabis is illegal for recreational purposes in many countries of the world, its use for medical purposes is recognized and allowed by law. Owing to these, there are products approved for investigational and medical purposes.

With respect to its usage mentioned above, both THC and CBD are often extracted from the plant itself. In some instances, synthesized versions of these cannabinoids are used instead of extracting them from the plant. Popular names in this area include: Sativex, Syndros, Dronabinol, Marinol etc. Epidiolex, for example, has been recently approved by the FDA to treat patients two years and older with seizures associated with Lennox-Gastaut syndrome (LGS) and Dravet syndrome. Epidiolex comes as an oral solution.

Recreational usage

When we say cannabis can be used for recreational purposes, what is meant is that it is used for reasons other than medical or spiritual. In other words, it is used just for the fun or pleasure of it. Recreational usage of cannabis goes as far back as the prehistoric periods. Through all ages, humans have been using cannabis for recreational purposes and this undoubtedly is the reason why cannabis followed people from one place to another. Invading armies brought it with them into the lands they were seeking to conquer and traders took it with them into virgin territories.

Recreational use of cannabis can be achieved through smoking but as discussed earlier, smoking is a more dangerous method of using cannabis. The wide availability of vaporizers has caused people to shift to vaporizing as a way of using cannabis for recreational purposes. Yet, there are still those who prefer the old ritual of enjoying cannabis as a joint, blunt or in a bong. It has been suggested that the availability of vaporizers is the reason why the clamor for legalizing cannabis for recreational purposes has increased in recent times and equally the same reason why legislatures all around the world are finding it easy to legalize it.

With the permissibility of recreational use of cannabis also comes the economic opportunity for manufacturers of edible products to make money. Therefore, since cannabis can be eaten or drunk, it has become part of the ingredients of many products that can be bought off the counter though in varying quantities. Also, users can make it part of the ingredients of the food they are cooking or a drink they are preparing.

Spiritual usage

Use of cannabis for spiritual purposes is perhaps the most ignored of its usages especially amongst its modern users. Spiritual use of cannabis also dates back to ancient times. There are numerous references in the religious scriptures and traditions of many ancient religions to how cannabis was being used in their religious activities. Perhaps a more detailed discussion of this is in order here.

Prominent amongst religious movements that accords cannabis a prominent place in their religious beliefs and practices is Rastafarianism. Rastafarianism is a religious movement that venerates the former emperor of Ethiopia, Haile Selassie. It also forbids the cutting of hair while stressing the black culture and identity. Ironically, though, cannabis is illegal in Ethiopia, the birthplace of the religion. In this religion, cannabis or marijuana, precisely, is used for the sacrament in place of the usual bread and wine.

In Shintoism, a religious belief system in Japan based on recognition and veneration of several gods and spirits associated with the natural world, cannabis holds a very important position. There is the need to keep off evil spirits from the body of a devotee and the way this is done is by the priest cleansing the devotees with hemp-laden sticks. At formal religious ceremonies, hemp robes are also worn.

Hinduism surely has its own use for cannabis as has been stated earlier in this book and so do the ancient Iranians who regarded it as the 'good narcotic' and consider it capable of inducing 'shamanic ecstasy'. Sufi Muslims also place some importance on cannabis in their mystical activities.

A question that has arisen in modern times as to the validity of the claim that cannabis can be used for spiritual purposes relates to how the many millions who use never get some kind of spiritual enlightenment as a result. A good answer to this is that actions are based on intentions – the focus has always been on the mind-numbing effect of cannabis rather than the mind-expanding qualities it has. It is like wielding a gun – you can terrorize with it or fight off aggression with it.

Other Economic Uses

There are other economic uses of cannabis that go beyond consumption. From the seeds of cannabis is produced Hash oil which is used as a paint. The plant itself has served, for many centuries, as a reliable source of fiber. In the past in England, for example, cannabis was grown mainly for its fiber for use in the English Navy and for other shipbuilding purposes. Other uses of cannabis in ancient times also include its use for making yarn from which clothes were made.

In modern times, cannabis is still used to make fiber and in fact this constitutes a major source of exchange for some countries. In places where cannabis is illegal for consumption whether for recreational or medical use, its use for other economic benefits is not prescribed by law. Hence, you can find the United Kingdom surprisingly topping the list of exporters of cannabis-based products.

Cannabis and the Law

There was a time most human societies cared little whether you were using cannabis or not. Whether you were using it for medical, recreational or spiritual purposes, society cared less. What changed? Society! As we came closer to modern times, human societies evolved into more sophisticated ones. Monarchies were replaced with secular democracies wherein the right to rule is not based on any divine right but rather being given the mandate to rule by the people through direct or indirect elections as dictated by constitutions, written or unwritten.

Society also changed in its perception of allowance and prohibition, and to this effect, laws come into existence to regulate the affairs of humans and punish offenders or violators. The attitude of society which once cared little about whether you were using cannabis suddenly changed to that of intolerance for the plant. This attitude of society to cannabis spread through the ancient routes of colonialism and even long after independence, former colonies have retained the attitude of their former masters or even surpassed them in strictness of regulation.

What makes this section of the chapter important is simply the fact that possession let alone use of cannabis can very well be a crime in many places. So, you can imagine what it will be like growing cannabis as far as the law is concerned. In succeeding paragraphs, I have attempted, to the best of my abilities, to relate the legal position of prominent countries on cannabis. Do not, however, take the information provided on this matter as legal counsel. The best thing to do is to in fact to consult a lawyer in your own country before you start dealing in cannabis. Or you may choose the well-trodden part of secret cultivation.

The US

The legal history of cannabis in the United States has been an interesting one. It went from something the state was less concerned with to being banned overnight in 1937 under the guise of an Act of the national legislature to tax the substance. This very likely led eventually to the removal of cannabis from the pharmacopeia of the United States in the mid-20th century. In 1970, the Controlled Substances Act was passed and cannabis became classified as a Schedule 1 drug. The effect of this was enormous – it meant cannabis had little medical use and great potential for abuse. This law was passed, in fact, in opposition to the recommendation of the committee appointed to investigate and report on the possible decriminalization of cannabis. The law would eventually slow down the rate of research on cannabis as it could not even be properly procured for research purposes.

However, efforts to legalize cannabis at the state level never stopped. Several groups sprang to mount pressure on the government to do the needful. In the same vein, experts keep clamoring for the removal of cannabis from Schedule 1 so as to promote proper research on it rather than just decriminalizing its use. At the moment, at least 29 states in the United States have decriminalized or legalized cannabis so that it only still remains a crime at the federal level.

Based on an amendment of the federal law against cannabis in states that legalized it, cultivation for medical purposes is safe from prosecution under the federal law. The federal law, however, does not provide the same protection for its recreational use though it seems enforcement is ignored in this regard. Another thing to note here is the difference between legalization and decriminalization. The former means there is no more law against it while the latter means it is treated as a minor infraction of the law which usually attracts punishments that are more like a slap on the wrist such as fines etc.

Also, there are differences from one state to the other when it comes to legalization whether for recreational or medical purposes; decriminalization; and legality of cultivation. Presently, 33 states have legalized cannabis for medical use though subject to a doctor's prescription. Recreational use of cannabis is only legal in 10 states and only 13 states have decriminalized it. Cultivation is allowed in about 22 states subject, however, to varying conditions such as the number of plants, commonly six with Alaska having the maximum of 12. Other conditions for cultivation include cultivation for medical purposes only and or with license and or within or outside the house. Only last year, President Trump signed into law a federal law permitting hemp, a plant variety that does not contain THC.

The UK

For the record, despite the fact that cannabis is illegal in the United Kingdom, the country still remains the largest exporter of legal cannabis i.e. cannabis low in THC, in the world. Cannabis became illegal in the UK in 1928 after the first law proscribing it was passed. However, its recreational use was still somehow allowed until the 1960s when its prevalence led to very stricter restrictions. This probably also led to its removal from the British Pharmacopoeia around the same time.

Historically, cannabis has remained a very important product in the English economy. In fact, there was a time land-owners in Britain had a legal obligation to grow cannabis and were subjected to penalties for not meeting their allotted quotas. This was undoubtedly due to the increasing demand for hempen ropes used majorly in the British Naval Fleet.

With the Misuse of Drugs Act of 1971 which made it a class B drug, the legal status of cannabis became one of total prohibition with prison sentences going as high as 5 years for simple possession and fourteen years in some cases. In effect, possession, distribution, cultivation etc. of cannabis is a crime in the UK. However, in order to allow the British Police focus on more important crime, attitude to enforcement is such that possession of little amount is waived provided the offender provides information to nail a bigger dealer. It seems cultivation for personal use in County Durham is overlooked though without legal backing, this is unsafe.

Canada

Canada was the first G7 country to legalize cannabis at the federal level. Cannabis became legalized in 2001 for medical purposes. However, Canadians would have to wait for 17 years before they could legally use cannabis for recreational purposes. Unlike the United States where the response to legalization is only at the state level, Cannabis is legal at the federal level in Canada subject, however, to provinces making additional regulatory provisions.

Particularly of interest to this book is the fact that cannabis can be home-grown in all the provinces in Canada except Quebec. Also, in places like Manitoba, cultivation is subject to medical license. Other regulatory provisions relating to the quantity that can be stored at home, whether it can be smoked in public, and at what age a person can legally use it. In all the provinces except Quebec and Manitoba which do not permit cultivation, the maximum number of plants you can cultivate is four.

China

In the People's Republic of China, Cannabis is illegal for both medical and recreational purposes. It is classified as a dangerous narcotic drug. Penalties for smoking it can though be detainment for up about 10-15 days and with fines. This is despite the fact that the plant might have originated right in China and the fact that historically, a part of China was famous for dealing in the plant.

Europe

There are varying regulations in other parts of Europe. In France, cannabis is illegal for recreational use though some cannabis-based drugs are permitted for medical use. In Italy, it is decriminalized for recreational purposes and strictly regulated for medical use. Cultivation is totally illegal and can be punished with imprisonment. In Spain, cultivation and use in private areas are allowed. While sale and importation are punishable with terms of imprisonment, any other thing done with it is treated as a misdemeanor and only attracts fines.

Africa

In most African countries, cannabis is outright illegal for recreational and medical use. In Nigeria, one of the world's major illegal users of cannabis, cannabis is outright illegal for both medical and recreational use. Prison terms may even include a life sentence. In South Africa, it is legal to use and cultivate cannabis privately. Medical use is also allowed but there are no systems of dispensing in this regard. In Egypt, the plant though occupied an important place in ancient Egyptian medical practices, is now illegal for both medical and recreational purposes. However, enforcement is largely ignored.

Asia and the Middle East

The case in Pakistan is the same as in Egypt – enforcement is largely ignored. In India, it is illegal for both medical and recreational use through enforcement is poor. However, an exception is made for Bhang, an edible preparation from cannabis that has been in use in

India for more than a thousand years now. There are state laws on this, though. In Israel, recreational use will become decriminalized in April, 2019 though it is completely legal for medical use. In Jordan, it is illegal for both medical and recreational use.

In this chapter, I have completed your introductory education on cannabis. I have opened your eyes to the interaction between cannabis and human society from the earliest of times to date. The history of cannabis has been presented to you and you will no doubt come to the conclusion that cannabis only started to be estranged from the millennia-old affection it had received from humans in the 19th to 20th centuries. From the loyal side-kick it was, to something that could cost your liberty, cannabis can very well boast, if it were human, to have witnessed the first-hand betrayal by man. However, that seems to be changing – societies now seem to be realizing their mistakes and are now taking appropriate steps to restore the plant to its once glorious status amongst humans.

CHAPTER 3

THE BASICS OF GROWING CANNABIS

The manner of growth of cannabis permits prospective gardeners to extensively lessen the expenses and simultaneously set up a compact rapport with the plant itself. Its brilliant adjustability, obtained via centuries of travel to the edges of the globe, gives it the ability to flourish and bloom anywhere there whether there may be daylight and water.

Through the process of studying the highly straightforward processes involved in gardening and spawning cannabis, you can keep far away from the unauthorized and illegal marketplace with its accompanying troubles. You can then focus on the development of the plant, bringing forth and utilizing the final manufactured product from one's personal hard work.

The Life Cycle of a Cannabis Plant and Photosynthesis

The cannabis is an annual plant that starts and completes its life cycle within a year. Usually, most plants mature in about six months. Others may take eight to nine months to mature. Luckily, cannabis can be grown all-round the year. Therefore, you can always start your cannabis farm at any period in the year.

There are six major stages in the growth of cannabis; germination, seedling, the vegetative pre-flowering, flowering and seed phases. Let's delve deeper into each.

Germination

This refers to the eruption and subsequent growth of the plant from the seed planted in the ground. The planted seeds take in water, the tissues of the embryo start to enlarge and ripen and tear the seed open along its suture. The radical root is the first to shoot out of the seed and it steers the growth earthward due to gravity. The shoot system of the seedling begins to also grow upwards as a form of taxis due to light. The shoot system reaches upward to access the sunlight required for growth. Once the seedling breaks the surface of the soil, a pair of embryonic leaves erupt and the shell of the seed is pushed away to leave the seedling anchored with its radical root. The embryonic leaves are small, and rounded; they contain green chlorophyll to absorb light for the emerging seedling. Germination takes place within as little as twelve hours to upwards of two or three weeks depending on the strain.

Seedling

Immediately after germination, the new seedling continues to produce new pairs of leaves. These are typically larger and possess the distinct three-rounded finger shape of cannabis plants and may possess jagged ends. They may be set on opposite sides of each other and sometimes, only one of the leaves is present. Some of these leaves may be very weak at the point of attachment to the growing stem and may require external support. With time, some of the older leaves also drop off. The seedling stage is concluded within two to six weeks.

Vegetative Growth

This is a stage where ultimate development takes place. The rate of growth of the plant is directly proportional to the energy that its leaves produce for the process of active development. Leaf tissues are manufactured each day and that increased the capabilities of development and growth. It is not uncommon to find a cannabis plant growing up to six inches in this phase per day. At the very least, a growth of one to two inches is usually observed at this stage. The stem of the plant becomes thicker, the leaves become firmer and stronger at its point of attachment. The number of blades on every leaf starts to reduce in the mid-process of the vegetative stage. After that, the placement of the leaves at the stem is altered from the regular opposite placement. The stem also begins to branch at this point. Vegetative growth is often completed in about five months.

Pre-flowering

The pre-flowering stage is an inactive extent of time of one to two weeks when the growth of the plant lags extensively. The plant is starting a brand new level of growth as encrypted in its DNA. There is a reduction in vertical growth. Instead, more branches and nodes are noticed. The plant attains a more robust appearance due to gradual filling out and calyxes where stems and branches meet appear.

Flowering

As I have mentioned before in the very first chapter, cannabis is a plant that has both male and female sexual parts in different plants. The male plants flower first before the female. However, for pollination to occur, it is important that the male plants be close to the female plants. Removal or absence of a male counterpart will cause the pollination process to falter.

In the male plants, little balls about a quarter inch in size and clustered together are formed. These contain the pollen grains. The female plant produces white stigmas raised upwards in the form of a 'V' shape and it is linked at the radical to an ovule which is blanketed in a very small green pod. The balls of the male plants eventually burst to release the pollen contained. Flowering normally takes up to one or two months to finish.

Seed Set

If fertilization has occurred, the female plants bear seed enclosed inside the green foliage of the plant. This continues to grow. If you are interested in gathering the seeds, then you need to pick them off at this moment before they burst open and are dispersed to the ground. Viable seeds take about ten days to five weeks to flourish.

During the flowering and seed set stages, several shades might also come into play. All of the plant's power goes into respawning and the multiplication of its species. Minerals and vitamins waft from the leaves to the seeds, and the chlorophylls that give the plant its green coloration decomposes.

Lighting

Adequate lighting is often the essential prop that indoor plants require. However, because they receive limited sunlight, artificial light is very important and vital. Plants demand the illumination to carry out the process of photosynthesis, the food-making process that is important for xylose and tissue manufacturing. A lot of individuals that develop the plant for individual use will make use of cupboard space for their nursery. You may even decide to make use of an empty room if you want to cultivate a large amount of cannabis. Nevertheless, you need to examine the liveliness, under the conditions of both free space and voltaic power, of delivering huge quantities of lighting. A lot of cannabis farmers restrict their preference to one of the following three alternatives: fluorescent lights, incandescent lights, and concealed (high-power discharge) lights.

To reduce your expenses, go for concealed lights or lamps for the duration of the vegetative and flowering period. Light is not really required for the cannabis seed to grow but further growth after the seed germinates requires additional lighting. Most growers flip the lights on after they sow the seeds to keep the soil heated and to speed up germination. The lights might also dry the outer part of the soil, particularly in large pots or with VHO fittings. If this poses an issue during the process of germination, turn off all the lights until you catch sight of the seedling poking out through the earth. Alternatively, suspend the lamp approximately eighteen inches above the soil, and bring it down to about six inches immediately the leaves begin to come out.

It is very vital for healthy growth that the plants receive a controlled night and day revolution. You can make use of an electronic electric timer which costs about eight dollars (you can find many of them on Amazon). A timer makes things so much simpler for you because you would not need to switch the lamps off or on each time by yourself. This would save you the stress of worrying about your plants during periods that you are not around such as short vacations. Set the timer to ensure that the plants get about sixteen to eighteen hours of light per day, and leave it this way until the seedlings have developed quite well.

The growing plants develop extra sluggishly with lesser than sixteen hours of artificial light per day, and they might produce prematurely. In cases where the plants have received too little light earlier on, some gardeners keep the lights on for whole days at a stretch. A phase longer than eighteen hours might speed up the rate of growth of the plant, particularly when the plants have not absorbed light to their full needs initially.

Also, pay attention to the intensity and heat generated by your chosen light source. The regular fluorescent lamps do not really get heated so much to scorch the plants unless they are in direct contact with the leaves for several hours. VHO conduits on the other hand will scorch the leaves even before they come in contact with them. Notwithstanding, the rule is to get the light as close to the plant as viable.

This allows for quick, strong and healthy bloom. Incandescent lights and flashlights get heated very quickly; place them at a farther range from the growing plant. Analyze the space between the light and the plant; ensure that you check for the intensity of the heat together with both of your hands. Put the bulb at the space where you start to experience its warmth. For a seventy-five watts glowing lamp, that is almost nearly eight inches.

In nurseries, whatever the source of the light might be, they should be placed as close as possible to the cannabis without scorching the plant. With accepted generated power tubes, hold the lights a maximum of two to six inches over the top of the plant. With VHO tubes, permit about four to eight inches above the plant. Hold the lamps at the given ranges through their lifetime in the nursery. Of course, you would need to heighten the lights as the plants grow taller.

Watering

Water is quite important for the internal processes in a plant; it gives hydrogen to aid the development of the plant. It is responsible for moving nutrients from one area to another. The quantity of water fed to the plant affects the growth rate. Too little water reduces the rate of growth of the plant and too much can clog up its roots. So, each plant type has its own optimal amount of water for it to grow.

For cannabis, it requires a fairly decent amount of water to grow but it does not thrive in damp, soaking or soggy soil. A common issue with growing your own cannabis therefore is overwatering the plants. This can occur when a plant is watered too many times in a short while. You have to understand that whenever you are watering the plant, ensure that the water makes the soil wet but does not get so much that it pools above the top layer of the soil. So, get the soil wet without allowing it to become soggy.

Soils versus Hydroponics

Soil

Of all the factors involved in growing cannabis and plants in general, the choice of soil is perhaps almost always the most important. Depending on how you handle the decision of which soil to use, you can be sure of a positive outcome or a negative one. Luckily, cannabis does not have a particular soil preference. It grows in a wide variety of soil types. You can grow different species of cannabis through a wide range of selection of soil. The most important soil factors are good drainage (to prevent water-logging), high presence of required nutrients and a pH close to neutral. With this in mind, here are some popular soil types and their viability or otherwise for growing cannabis

Types of Soil

Different soils are composed of different constituents such as sand, muck, clay, silt and loam in different quantities. These constituents give each soil type the peculiarities that make them favorable/unfavorable for cannabis cultivation.

Sandy Soils

Sandy soils are made from rocks that have gone through disintegration over a long period of time, usually rocks which have been made from sediments. The soil has the ability to drain water quite well but a consequential effect is that it has some difficulty holding liquid and nutrients which seep away as soon as the soil is being watered. A few soils of this kind are very fruitful, the reason being that they have a large number of organic materials which also hold a large amount of water. Sandy soils are abundant in magnesium, potassium and trace elements. However, they are quite deficient in phosphorus and very deficient in nitrogen. They also retain sheet compost quite well. To use sandy soil for cannabis cultivation, you must be careful enough to select soil that can retain water better than most sandy soils. You can supplement this with sheet compost to make them even better for the purpose you have in mind.

Silts

This is another kind of soil composed of majorly quartz and some other minerals along with loose organic matter. They are created as a product of deposition from flooding of earthly land, lagoons and rivers. On examination when they are wet, they resemble slimy clay and when they are dry, they look like a darker shade of sand. Silts are capable of holding liquid or moisture but they also lose water well. Silts have the richest nutrients and they usually allow for active and quick growth of plants as a result of a rich supply of nitrogen.

Muck

These kinds of soil are created in locations with sufficient amount of rain which has a large cover of trees and plants. Usually, their acidic content is very high but they are fertile. They are low in potassium and there are varying densities of this type of soil. The thicker kinds of soils require the need to be prepared for cultivation by plowing and harrowing. However, the less thick forms of muck can be cultivated in heaps. Muck often holds water really well. So, if you select this soil for cannabis cultivation, then you need to be extra careful while watering your plants to avoid excess water.

Clay Soils

Clay soils are made up of smooth and lucid particles that have been brought about by gradual chemical reaction among the minerals. They dry easily and they release water weakly. This form of soil is not advisable for the growing of cannabis because the roots of the plant have a difficult time stretching through the soil as it dries quickly unless the clay soil has been tilled properly. Usually, they are fertile and the relationship between the plant and the soil depends on the drainage system of the soil which unfortunately is not too good for cannabis cultivation.

Loamy Soil

Loamy soils are generally a mix of silt, sand and clay in a rough percentage of 40:40:20 respectively. They contain organic content and that makes them suitable for the growth of cannabis. They require very little modification to support the development of a healthy cannabis garden. Of all soil types, they also exhibit the kind of water retention that is most optimal for cannabis growth.

These are the different types of soil and how they may work out for your plants but the soil is not the only medium for growing plants.

Hydroponics

In the early days of agriculture, soil used to be the major growth medium for plants but then, researchers have come to realize that for a plant to grow, it only needs any medium capable of providing support, nutrients, drainage and allow air to get to the roots. Now, soil did all these but at times, planting in the soil can also throw up a pretty good challenge or problem. Some soils do not drain well and it is also a lot harder to realize that there are problems with your plant. Most times, you do not even realize the problem until it starts to show in the leaves or stem. By which time it may be too late to rescue your precious plant. Also, it is a lot harder to decide just how much nutrients to feed your plants because with soil, you do not know what type and amount of nutrients are available. These problems gave rise to hydroponics as a suitable replacement for soil.

Therefore, as Greg Green describes it, hydroponics "is the technique of growing plants without soil, but rather in beds of sand, gravel, or artificial mediums that are flooded with a nutrient solution". In essence, a hydroponics system consists of a pot or container, growth medium, pump, and nutrients.

The container is divided into layers; the top layer holds the growth medium where the plant is grown. After germination, the roots of the seedling grow downward into the lower layer where water and nutrients are. A pump connected to this layer helps regulate the movement and concentration of the nutrients.

With hydroponics, there is faster growth as the plant is able to direct its energy and metabolic process to upwards growth rather than devote some of them to the downwards movement of roots through the soil. In fact, the growth of roots in a hydroponic setup is so rapid that it may threaten to be a problem even.

Aside from this, hydroponics systems also cost way more than using soil. Therefore, if you are growing a sizable number of plants, using hydroponics can add significant extra costs to your overhead. The system also requires a constant supply of fresh water and a balanced nutrient concentration at all time. If this balance is disturbed even for a few hours, it can have lasting effects on your plants.

Some common examples of hydroponics include;

Deep-water Culture

The deep-water culture method also referred to as the reservoir method, is the easiest process of growing your plant with hydroponics. In this system, the roots are hung in a solution of nutrients and an air pump system allows oxygen into the solution of nutrients. You need to prevent rays of light from touching the system though because this will support the growth of algae.

Nutrient Film Technique

NFT allows the continuous movement of the solution of nutrients through the roots of the plant. The solution is angled a little so that the solution of the nutrients will move in the direction of gravity.

Ebb & Flow

The ebb and flow hydroponics system works by flooding the location where the plant is required to grow with the solution of nutrients at given periods. With time, the solution of nutrients then seeps back into the tank. The pump comes with a timer so that the nutrients can be given to the plant's as required.

In conclusion, when it comes to choosing the right soil for your cannabis plant, your focus should be on the selecting a soil with the right proportion of organic matter, good water retention and draining capacity and a soil structure that can support the growth of your plants. A hydroponic system is another option you should consider. It allows your plant to grow faster and produce a better yield. However, it is more cost and labor intensive for a beginner. So, the choice is yours.

Nutrients

In the life and development of plants, fifteen elements are important to aid their growth. From water and air, we can easily get carbon, oxygen and hydrogen readily. The other twelve essential elements are obtained mainly from the earth in inorganic forms like nitrate and potassium ion. They form a part of the soil that gets accessible to plants when organic content rots and forms particles in the soil mix. These elements are needed by soil for adequate growth and support of your cannabis plants. The major nutrients which are required for the healthy growth of your plant include Nitrogen, Potassium and Phosphorus. These elements are sometimes concentrated in fertilizers and sold under the name "N-P-K". The fertility of a particular soil is estimated by the quantity of nitrogen, potassium and phosphorus in the soil.

Calcium, Sulphur and Magnesium are referred to as the secondary or macronutrients. Usually, plants do not need these nutrients in large quantities and almost all soils contain these nutrients.

Trace or Macronutrients consist of six elements which are required in very little quantity. Soils which are utilized for the commercial uses contain these nutrients too in sufficient amount.

Nitrogen

Cannabis is regularly referred to as a plant which loves nitrogen. The higher the quantity of nitrogen in the soil, the higher the fertility it has.

Nitrogen is required in almost all part of the growth cycle that takes place in the cannabis plant. In the makeup of amino acids, nitrogen is a very important element. As long as your cannabis plants get a sufficient supply of nitrogen, they will grow very well. A sufficient supply of nitrogen leads to quick and delightful growth. Therefore, you need to supplement nitrogen if your soil is deficient in this element.

Phosphorous

Phosphorus is a component of NADP and ATP that generate energy in biological structures. It is also a constituent of the genetic makeup. It is important for photosynthesis and respiration to take place. Cannabis utilizes a lot of phosphorus during the stages of germination and seedling. It is also very important during the stage of flowering and seed setting.

Potassium

Potassium controls a lot of processes in the plant system like respiration, photosynthesis, synthesis of proteins etc. Potassium also works to confer some degree of immunity against disease in your plant.

Calcium

Calcium works to speed up the fusion of fatty mixtures and the membranes of cells. It is also very important in the reproduction and replication of the cells. Cannabis requires a lot of calcium more than it normally does to help with an active growth cycle. It can be served to the cannabis plant to fine-tune the soil's acid levels.

Sulfur

In some proteins and amino acid, sulfur can be found. It is a substantial part of the vitamins in plants like aneurin which is important for healthy metabolism. Soils suitable for the development and growth of cannabis should have a lot of sulfur content

Magnesium

Magnesium is a participant in the absorption of carbohydrates and in the fusion of proteins. It is an important element in the makeup of the molecules of chlorophyll and thus very vital to the process of photosynthesis.

Trace Elements

The trace elements include Iron, Magnesium, Manganese, Boron, copper and zinc and they are essential in speeding up the growth and development process of the plant. As explained before, the cannabis plant utilizes them in only small quantities but it is absolutely vital that they be present for healthy growth. They facilitate a lot of life processes like the breaking down and building up of molecules. Deficiency of any of the vital elements can lead to stunted and poor growth.

Temperature, Humidity and Air Quality

Temperature

The temperature of the room where the plant is being grown needs to be checked and controlled from time to time. The regular condition for a cannabis garden should be about 75°F. With all that said, cannabis is very adaptable to several temperatures and will survive and continue to thrive under a high or low temperature although the quality of the cannabis may be highly affected. The plants grow a little better at higher temperatures but these temperatures might be difficult to keep up with so it is better to stick with a particular temperature.

Humidity

For sufficient growth and budding, the relative humidity in your cannabis garden should be about forty to eighty percent. Humidity can simply be explained as the estimation of the amount of moisture in the air. It is advisable to make use of a dehumidifier to regulate the level of humidity in the garden.

Carbon Dioxide (CO_2)

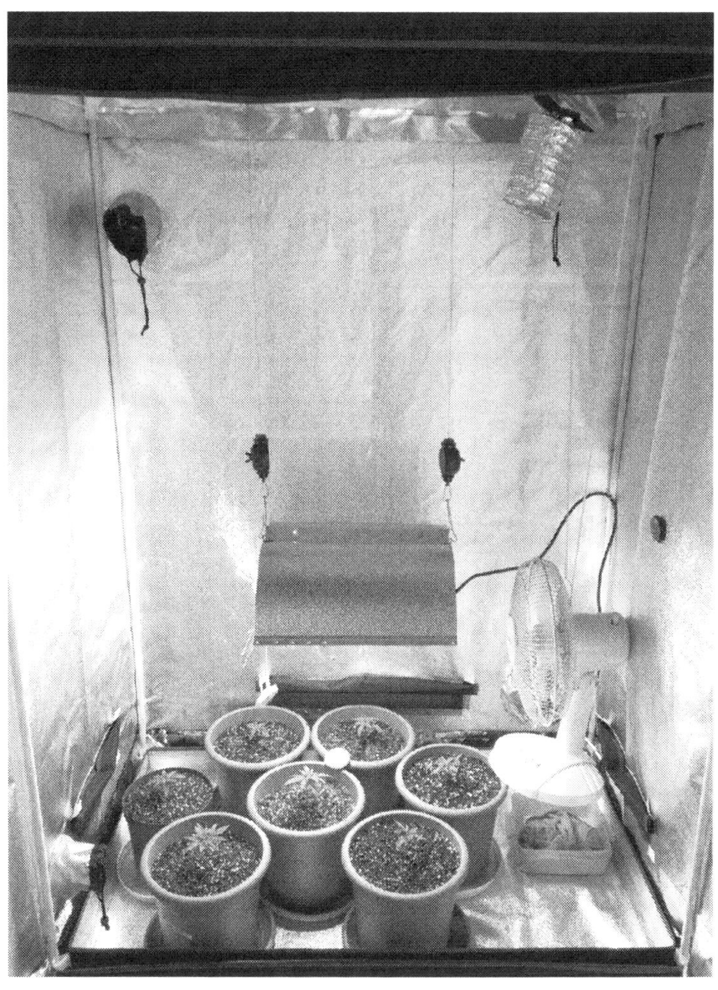

Carbon dioxide or CO_2 is a very important element needed for the plant to survive. Carbon dioxide can be increased in a room with the help of a CO_2 generator, it will release a continuous flow of carbon dioxide into the grow room and that will allow the plants to breathe easily. Otherwise, the amount of carbon dioxide in the room is directly proportional to how large the plant (and eventually the buds) will end up growing. There is no known way of overloading your cannabis plants with carbon dioxide. There is never too much

Where is the best place to grow cannabis?

Cannabis grows well enough outdoors but the witch-hunt against it means you may probably not want to grow outdoors. Instead, for most people, indoor cultivation is easy enough and safe for their preoccupation with cannabis.

Choosing to grow your cannabis indoors poses yet another question. There are different ways of adapting an indoor system for cannabis cultivation. So, which one do you go for? Of course, the primary advantage of growing cannabis indoors is safety and security from prying eyes. There are three main options available to you in terms of indoor cultivation; a tent, room or grow box (cabinet). Let us look at their individual merits and demerits.

Growing cannabis under a tent may not necessarily be wise as a tent is hardly the most secret place to keep it away from exposure. Besides, it is a lot harder to control lighting conditions under a tent. However, tents offer a larger expanse of space to grow more cannabis plants.

Growing cannabis in a room does offer more security than an outdoor tent but also needs further security measures to be put in pace. You do not want unwanted visitors barging into the room to find a thriving cannabis garden. That may come across as awkward and is definitely unsafe for your concealment. You will also need to find a way to cover windows from possible prying eyes. A room however offers you a great deal of control over the conditions. You may need to rig out a lighting system to bring the lights closer to your plants but there is no doubt that it is easier to do in a room.

Using a grow box though is perhaps the best way to cultivate your cannabis indoors. Think of the benefits of using a room minus all the disadvantages. That is what a grow box gives you. It is essentially a small cabinet or an enclosed tent that can be brought indoors. A grow box offers you more privacy and control over variable factors. Humidity and temperature can be easily controlled and you can get to place adjustable lights within your grow box. As depicted in the picture above, you can even paint the inner walls of your box to reflect light better onto your precious plants.

CHAPTER 4

BASIC CANNABIS KNOWLEDGE: GENOTYPE AND PHENOTYPE

What are Strains and Why do they Matter?

Cannabis strains are varieties of the cannabis plant cultivated for specific qualities or characteristics. Strains are varieties of the different species of the cannabis plant, sativa, indica and ruderalis. These varieties are usually named to reflect characteristics of the particular strain such as its size, odor or origin.

Strains may also differ in their primary intended use. Even though most strains are grown for recreational and medical usages as we have discussed in the first chapter, others have other economic purposes such as the production of hemp and oils for various uses.

The two most commonly grown cannabis species are Cannabis indica and Cannabis sativa as they are both useful for recreation and medical purposes. Cannabis ruderalis, the other common species is less commonly grown as it doesn't offer any such uses. Rather, it is often used in developing hybrid seeds for growing.

The different strains of cannabis develop from these three species. On the one hand, as much as fifteen wild strains of cannabis is found on average growing wildly in most countries. Beyond natural selection though. Humans have dabbled extensively into crossbreeding different strains to select particularly desirable end products rich in certain taste, odor or even quality of the highness it confers. For instance, in some countries where cannabis is only allowed to be farmed for fabrics production, strains are genetically modified such that it contains very little or even no THC.

These genetically modified strains have several advantages over pure or wild strains. First, they have a growing history. Therefore, it is easy to trace their survival rates and get better information on their possible peculiarities. Their suppliers can give you a whole lot of background information that will keep you better informed about what you need to be doing.

Also, through trial and error, strains are often produced based on specific desirable qualities that they possess. You may want to check online for the particular strain that meets your own desired needs before you select one to plant. Therefore, whether your overall intention is to grow or consume, there is a strain out there that has been customized just to suit you. You just need to take a moment out to find it. Some more common cannabis strains include Acapulco gold, bedrocan, blue dream, charlotte's web, purple kush, tom cruise purple, skunk, and sour diesel.

Sativa

The sativa species was first identified and classified by *Carl Linnaeus*. In appearance, sativa often grows taller (4-15 feet) than its indica counterpart, and its leaves are generally larger but narrower, with fewer or no markings. It has long internodes within its branches stretching up to six inches in some cases. Most sativa plants are either male or female with very few being hermaphrodites.

Merits

Cannabis sativa does have plenty of uses. Among the multitudes of benefits of cannabis sativa to humans are:

- Weight loss: cannabis users have been observed to be slimmer than non-users. This is no coincidence, as the plant is known to help regulate insulin production and optimize caloric intake.

- Fights cancer: certain cannabinoids found in cannabis sativa, cannabinoids have been found by scientists to combat several kinds of cancer or at least reduce the risk percentage of developing these cancers.

- Prevents diabetes: due to its weight loss and insulin regulation function, the plant helps to prevent the onset of diabetes.

- Antidepressant: depression is one of the more endemic, yet less talked about mental health disorder in the world today. Research has shown that cannabis can help relieve people suffering from this condition by improving their moods.

- Seizure regulation: Using medical cannabis sativa to regulate seizures is another one of the high-profile findings coming out of medical science. For people with brain conditions such as epilepsy, cannabis can alleviate the most severe symptoms.

- Pain management: the THC in cannabis sativa has an astounding capacity to reduce pain and discomfort.

Demerits

The cannabis sativa plant does come with some potentially negative effects too. Some of these are:

- The THC in cannabis sativa can cause or increase dizziness, paranoia, and anxiety.

- Sativa strains, especially those that are high in THC, can cause headache and nausea.

- One of the less severe negative effects of consuming cannabis is dryness of the eyes and mouth. These symptoms, though uncomfortable, are usually mild and easily manageable.

- It can induce and increase mental illness. Especially for youths whose brains are still growing and developing, cannabis consumption can have negative effects on the brain. These changes in brain chemistry can develop into an increase in depression and anxiety, leading to sadness, grief, sleeping and eating disorders, and so forth. Additionally, smoking is a bad habit, and often this is the way that cannabis is consumed, meaning that its regular intake can develop into a lasting bad habit. The good thing is smoking is not the only way to enjoy your sativa.

- Sativa plants are often large, with thick stems and do not lend itself well to secret cultivation.

Indica

There is some general debate as to whether Cannabis indica is truly a distinct species or a form of sativa. Notwithstanding, the consensus is that indica has sufficient enough distinguishing features to be called a distinct species. Described by Bismarck who named it "indica" to show its origin (close to India), Cannabis indica is a much smaller plant than sativa species. It rarely rises above four feet, and fully grown indica plants less than eight feet in height have been found. However, indica plants grow much faster and produce more yield than sativa. It also has shorter nodes of less than three inches, and its rounded leaves bear visible markings.

Merits

- Cannabis indica can be used to lighten mood due to its effect on dopamine, a neurotransmitter in the body. Dopamine is referred to as the happiness hormones as it is responsible for the feeling of joy. Indica typically induces a higher level of dopamine in the body.

- It can also be used to relieve pain

- Derivatives of indica such as Marinol and Cesamet can be used to deal with episodes of nausea and vomiting in cancer patients.

- Cannabis indica can also sharpen the appetite

- Indica can also function as a muscle relaxant

- The plant has been proven to be useful for patients with sleep problems including insomnia

- Cannabis indica has been observed to be effective against depression

Demerits

- It causes sleepiness and drowsiness
- Users of cannabis indica usually have to deal with poor judgment and forgetfulness in the immediate moments after use.

Comparison Table between Indica and Sativa

Below is a table that contrasts the major differences between cannabis sativa and cannabis indica:

Cannabis Sativa	Cannabis Indica
Has lower levels of THC compared to CBD	Has higher levels of THC as compared to CBD
Grows taller and slimmer	Grows shorter and bushier
Have long leaves with long thin blades	Have wide, short leaves with short wide blades
Sativa strains are likely to be long, sausage-shaped flowers	The buds of indica strains tend to be wide, and dense
Cannabis sativa has lower levels of THC to CBD.	Cannabis indica has higher levels of THC compared to CBD
Produces a more vivid and uplifting "high."	produces sedative effects, possesses a more calming, soothing, and numbing experience

Sativas are uplifting and cerebral, enhancing creativity and productivity.	Indicas tend to decrease energy
Produce more of a "mind high."	Produce what has been called a "body high
Sativa plants require longer to grow and yield fewer active ingredients	Indica plants require a shorter time to grow and yield more active ingredients

How to Choose Your Strain

The underlying factor behind choosing what cannabis strain to consume is the popular belief about the effects individual strains have upon the mind and body of the consumer. Cannabis sativa, for example, is believed to be more of an energizer, while indicas are widely believed to have a relaxing effect. It is logical, therefore, that most people consume sativa strains when they need a boost in energy, or when undertaking a mentally taxing activity. On the other hand, indica strains are mostly used for calming or soothing properties, such as in dealing with insomnia.

Despite the widespread belief about the effects of different strains of cannabis, there is a dearth of scientific studies backing up the assertion that a particular cannabis strain would consistently provide a "known" kind of effect or reaction. This is to say, in essence, that although sativas are believed to be the 'cerebral' strains and indicas are the 'mellow' ones, one should not expect all sativas to be mentally uplifting and all indicas to be calming and relaxing. The effects generated from the use of a particular strain of cannabis are copious and unpredictable and depend largely upon the strain's and consumer's genetic architecture, as well as the strain's chemical constituents.

Further on chemical constituents, there are tens of them in each strain of cannabis out there. The most common and significant of these can be grouped under two families, namely terpenes and cannabinoids.

Terpenes are the chemical compounds that give each cannabis strain its unique smell and taste. They are produced by certain plants as a protective oil to both help ward off insect pests as well as serve a reproductive function.

Cannabinoids are the chemicals that are responsible for the psychoactive effects of cannabis. They are secreted by the cannabis plant primarily to act as a defense agent against invading pests. There are at least 113 cannabinoids in every cannabis plant, occurring in various compositions and quantities.

Together, terpenes and cannabinoids are better markers of the effects to expect from a cannabis strain. Depending on the relative amounts of cannabinoids and terpenes present, a cannabis strain will either produce the infamous psychoactive 'high' effect or a more calming, soothing effect.

Each strain of cannabis you consume is going to provide you with a different experience. Therefore, in choosing the strain you are going to consume, due diligence and research are required. If you are growing for your individual need, then you should also be aware that even for the same strain, effects can differ from one individual to another.

CHAPTER 5

GERMINATE SEEDS

Types of Cannabis Seeds, Merits and Demerits

Germinating cannabis seeds is one of the most important topics in the cannabis growing process, and, to the newbie grower, a panacea to pick up invaluable knowledge. Tons of seeds are processed and sold by various manufacturers today, each with its unique offers and qualities. There are three types of cannabis seeds. They are:

A. Feminized seeds

Feminized cannabis seeds have been bred by top cannabis outlets over the last generation to have no male parts and when grown, produce about a 95% ratio of female plans to male plants. Feminized seeds have over time become a worthy alternative to regular cannabis seeds. A major reason why these seeds have garnered much recognition lies in the fact that investing in them makes the entire process of growing cannabis less labor intensive. Typically, when regular seeds are utilized (a combination of male and female seeds), sprouted male plants are removed to make more room for the more useful female plants. Using feminized seeds yanks out this step, as only female plants are obtained, thus saving energy and costs.

With the absence of male plants, female plants can grow larger and produce bigger buds. Due to the fastidious genetic section process that produced them, feminized seeds have been known to produce their buds independent of male pollination.

Conditions for germinating feminized seeds, such as light and heat, are not as strict as those commanded by regular seeds; in essence, using from used seeds comes with a lot of ease.

In summary, feminized seeds are well suited to growers who are either low on cultivation space or want to save energy by eliminating the male-cutting step. Also, feminized seeds are known to produce high amounts of effective cannabinoids. Therefore, if you want good cannabis for less effort and time, feminized seeds are the way to go.

B. Autoflowering seeds

Autoflowering seeds are similar to feminized seeds, as they too do not require such intensive care and germinating conditions as are required by regular seeds, and mature relatively early. These seeds have been found to mature in about ten weeks.

Autoflowering seeds are so named because they have a proclivity for sprouting flowers automatically, one of their most desired properties. Another desirable feature of these seeds is the stout nature of the plants they produce, which makes them easy to maintain. Like feminized seeds, autoflowering seeds also do not require the elimination of male plants. Thus, they are also a less-effort variety of seeds.

They have also been in existence long before feminized seeds. However, because they used to be typically low in strength, breeders have increased the active agents with a genetic selection such that they are now as strong and potent as regular seeds.

C. Regular Seeds

Before feminized and auto-flowering seeds were developed, there were just the regular seeds which were roughly 50% male and 50% female. As a result, the yield was 50/50. So, double the work was needed to get the same amount of cannabis.

Experienced growers often advocate and root for regular seeds. However, if this is your first foray into cannabis cultivation, I advise you to go for feminized seeds as they're easier to work with. Regular seeds require more attention and care in terms of lighting and temperature, and of course, time and energy must be invested in removing the male plants and cultivating the female instead after pollination.

Deciding Which Seed to Choose

Choosing the right seed to plant can be quite confusing for a beginner. Therefore, you need to research the best possible seeds for you before you decide.

Choosing the Right Strain

We have already discussed the importance of choosing the right strain, but this cannot be overstated. Spend as much time as needed to come to a decision about which strain of cannabis matches well with your vision and needs. Consider the space you have and the reason you are planting cannabis in the first place. For instance, if you have a very small and limited space for growing cannabis, you may want to go for strains of the indica species as they are generally smaller in size. Choosing the right strain can make or mar your cultivation even before you have started.

Price

Different strains of different qualities have a huge difference in price. The amount itself, however, does not necessarily translate into quality. However, shop around the limited supplies you potentially have and come to terms with a seed that offers you decent quality without creating a dent in your budget. This is only the beginning to remember. You are still going to spend more money setting up your plants.

Caring for Seedlings

Seedlings are prime targets for destruction by insects, pests, rodents, and pathogen. This is potentially more destructive since seedlings have a smaller surface area and are less able to repel these attacks compared to full-grown plants. Therefore, the onus is on the grower to provide adequate shelter for the young seedlings.

These days, many cannabis farmers cut transparent, plastic bottles in half and place the same over their growing plants. Holes are usually left in the bottom of these cut bottles for adequate aeration. The cut bottle can, therefore, serve effectively as a guard against pests and further insulation against sudden changes in temperature.

Just like full-grown plants, your seedlings also require certain factors to promote their healthy growth and promote their chances of reaching maturation faster. Of these, sunlight and water are critical. Most of the other variables for your seedlings are the same as the overall needs of the cannabis plant as I have already discussed. However, I will run through some of them with an emphasis on their effect on seedlings.

Water

It is important to provide enough water for your seedlings. You can check if the soil is wet enough for them by dipping a finger into the soil around their roots to test for moistness. Another effective way for checking this is by noticing if the soil you planed your plant in, refuses to stick to the walls of the pot it is contained due to dryness. This is often a sure signal for you to water your plants. Underwatering if noticed in time can be dealt with easily by simply wetting your plants.

However, it is also possible to overwater your plants if care is not taken. This is even harder to detect as it shares the same signs as Underwatering. To prevent this, always do the finger check on the soil around your seedling before you add more water. If the soil is still moist, hold off the watering a little longer.

Nutrients

An overabundance of nutrients can pose negative effects to cannabis plants especially the smaller ones. Too many nutrients can fire in a negative direction by causing a lack of absorption and diminished nutrition for your seedling. You must, however, be careful not to starve your seedlings of the required nutrients or lead them into an acute nutrient deficiency state. This can happen to your seedlings and plants irrespective of whether they are grown in soil or hydroponics. So, you must remain vigilant always.

Temperature

The consensus about the right temperature for healthy seedlings is around 75 degrees Fahrenheit. You do not want your seedlings getting baked in hotter temperatures than this. A telltale sign of too high a temperature is that the leaves begin to curl. This often frequently happens when the lighting system has been placed too close to the seedlings. Therefore, you can simply ease back the light and save your seedlings.

Lighting

Adequate sunlight is a must. Plants bend towards the nearest source of light when they do not get enough light. If you deprive your seedlings of enough light, they will grow a horizontal bend that is not desirable. Artificial lights can save you from these if your seedlings aren't receiving enough sunlight especially if you have planted them indoors in the first place. Fluorescent lights are generally good for seedlings because it barely forces the temperature the seedlings are being exposed to above the required range. You can keep this on for eighteen to twenty hours a day. This applies for seedlings grown outdoors as well.

You can refer back to chapter three for more insight about these factors as both seedlings and mature plants share similar requirements and challenges.

CHAPTER 6

HOW TO START A MOTHER PLANT

What is a Mother Plant?

Not all cannabis plants have to start life as a seed or go through the germination process. Instead, cannabis can also be propagated asexually from a mother plant. What are mother plants?

A mother plant is a healthy female cannabis plant bred up to vegetative level and then prevented from going into flowering. From these non-reproducing females, several cuttings are made that can then be replanted to grow as clones of the mother plants. These clones will grow to possess the same traits as the mother plant they are taken from because they have the same genetic makeup.

This type of propagation of cannabis plants is known as asexual propagation as it does not require fertilization of a female plant by pollen grains from a male plant. Instead, the female plant itself is cut and replanted to give rise to identical clone plants.

Cannabis mother plants are carefully selected by cultivators because they possess favorable features, such as the ability to produce big yields; a resistance to disease; the ability to flourish in a specific cultivation environment (such as indoors or in a greenhouse), or the taste, smell, and effect of the flowers they produce. Cannabis mother plants are usually strong, vigorous plants that are deliberately kept in their vegetative state to produce clones that grow and develop quickly.

Mother plants are treasured favorites of growers who often isolate them from the rest of the growing field. They are preserved for these favorable traits and then regrown to keep the traits safe.

Asexual propagation of cannabis, therefore, has certain obvious advantages over the natural, sexual process. Like other asexual propagation methods such as grafting, layering, and budding, using a mother plant is faster than planting seeds as about two stages in the typical lifecycle are bypassed entirely. However, most growers who use mother plants do so to foster familiarity and bring forth assured traits that are desired.

Nobody wants to lose a good mother plant, especially when she has all of the characteristics that are considered desirable in a cannabis plant. An easy way of ensuring that these desirable characteristics are enjoyed over a long period is by taking cuttings from the mother plant. As clones taken from a mother plant are exact replicas of their mother, the grower is guaranteed to have an all-female, desirable cannabis yield.

Using mother plants also offer you the luxury of familiarity with your crops especially if it is not your first time. Since you already have a good idea of the requirement of the other plant, and you know the clones are going to have the same needs, and you have a better handle on things. It also gives you the chance to experiment with definitive results. For instance, varying the amount of light and nutrients that identical clones get while monitoring their rate of growth will give you conclusive data about the right amount of light and nutrients for subsequent plants you grow.

With a good mother plant, your cannabis growing experience can be easily manipulated to suit your personal needs and expectations.

How to Decide a Mother Plant

Mother plants are themselves propagated sexually through pollination. Many times even, they are accidentally discovered during growth. For instance, if you come across a particularly strong female plant that seems to embody many desirable traits, you may not wish to lose these traits as will undoubtedly occur at harvest. Therefore, a grower may choose to retain these traits by cloning more plants with the same desirable characteristics.

You need to be logical and rational while choosing a mother plant though. For instance, it makes no sense to select a plant that has suffered damage from pests and pathogens before. Even if it has survived the attack, that may mean it is genetically susceptible to that pathogen. Since it is going to pass on this trait to its clones, choosing such a plant as a mother plant may render your cultivation an exercise in futility.

Also, regardless of how strong or viable a mother plant is, get ready to change or discard it after a maximum of two growing seasons. It will grow weaker as time goes on and cellular degradation occurs. It will start to produce weaker clones as well.

You also need to create space for your mother plant where it can thrive under a vegetative phase. Obviously, due to the different requirements, this cannot be the same area you keep your flowering plants.

It is of absolute importance also that you keep very accurate records of which clones belong to what mother plants. That will allow you to form several, correct conclusions at the end and save you the stress that confusion can bring in.

You can even number your clones and keep photos detailing each step of the process. That way, you have a kind of journal to refer to always.

When deciding which plant to call your mother plant, you should consider the following steps:

Use regular seeds

It is easier to use feminized seeds as they reduce the level of uncertainty, but most experienced growers choose mother plants only from regular seeds. Using feminized seeds brings an attendant risk of hermaphroditism where male flowers suddenly begin to grow as well on the plant. This may happen as a result of the extra stress mother plants often undergo and is more common in feminized seeds.

Use F1 hybrid seeds

Usually, growers tend to like to keep their mother plants that they have bred. The consensus seems to be that F1 hybrids produced as the first generation of a cross between two parents are the best bets for creating a mother plant. Mother plants grown from F1 seeds seem to undergo natural selection which leaves them with a large pool of traits to pick from both parents. This strong genetic advantage has been fingered as being responsible for the faster growth rates they exhibit.

If you do not have access to F1 hybrid seeds though, your next best bet is to go for F2 hybrids gotten from the combination of two different F1 hybrid seeds. This breeding process, however, is time intensive. Imagine having to plant the parents and wait for them to provide the F1 hybrid seeds. If you are into the cultivation of cannabis as a leisure activity or hobby, it can prove to be too complex a process for you. Add to that the fact that not everyone can source F1 hybrids and you get a better idea of the scope of the task ahead.

However, using F1 hybrids is not completely compulsory. If you cannot find them, use the regular seeds too and pay close attention to them growing.

Make your selection

This is the less physically stressful part of the whole task. The moment your prospective choices for a mother plant begin to flower, you need to start checking them out to determine the eventual ones that are good enough for your requirements as a mother plant. Most experienced growers advise that you look for qualities such as;

- Strength: a mother plant is going to go through a lot of stress. Therefore, they should be healthy, robust plants that grow well. Choosing a strong mother plant will give you the chance to take cuttings for longer before it needs to be replaced. Look out for signs of rude health in the vegetative phase

- Appearance: you may have certain desirable traits you have in mind in terms of size and structure of your plants. If this is so, then you need to pick a plant that has visible signs of meeting your requirements. For instance, if your garden is indoors, you may prefer plants with a shorter space span that are easy to conceal from prying eyes. Some other growers prefer the larger plants. It is a case of different strokes for different folks. You get to make your choice of what your eventual product is going to be.

- Yield: Yield is obviously the end-target for all growers. Depending on what you want, you should be able to sense what plants will make great mother plants for your need. Whether you are more concerned about the size and quantity of cannabis you produce, or you are more particular about the grade and quality, your choice of mother plant is key.

- Aroma: Cannabis growers have varied interest in the aroma of their plants. Luckily, cannabis plants have enough types of aromas to satisfy us all. Choose a mother plant from among the plants whose aroma satisfy your yearnings best. However, it is best advised that you select a mother plant whose aroma is not too strong to call for unnecessary attention.

Deciding on your choice of plant for your mother plant is a factor of your likes both as a user and cannabis farmer. Your best friend in this decision is your eyes. Look at and observe your plants well before you finally select one.

Basic Steps to Starting a Mother Plant

The first step in growing a mother plant is selecting a favorable seed and strain. It is best to start mother plants from seeds as plants grown sexually from seeds have a stronger root system to keep them firmly anchored and stronger for longer.

After germination, allow your plants to grow up to the vegetative state. By the third week of the vegetative phase, sex differentiation has already started. Male plants begin to acquire sacs, and the females start to form stigmas. You can remove the male patients and select the strongest looking females to serve as your mother plants.

Let's dive straight into the steps of cutting a clone out. Materials required for cloning include razor, water-containing container (a glass container would do just fine here), rooting hormone, dome (to provide appropriate humidity levels), a pair of scissors, and the medium that would hold the clones. I prefer a razor blade because it accounts better for the delicateness of the clone to be cut. A pair of scissors is harder to control and could end up crushing some part of the clone.

If you are planning to use hydroponics, then you can use rapid rooters or rock wool cubes as your growing medium. You can just plant your fresh clone cuttings in them. Set up the humidity dome as well before you place your developing clones in it so that the conditions in the grow tent are already at an optimum before your clones come in. Aim for a high humidity level and temperatures of around 75 degrees Fahrenheit. They should also be receiving 18 hours of light each day, so they continue to grow.

How to Keep a Mother Plant

The mother plant is often the most treasured plant in your little cannabis garden. As complex and time-consuming as it may be to find the right mother plant, it is of importance to keep this plant alive and viable for as long as possible. As the potential donor of many more other plants, it is essential that it receives the due attention it deserves.

It is recommended that you follow these steps religiously to keep your mother plant alive and well:

1) Select a big container to house your mother plant. Or you can go for a good hydroponics system. An example is the GH Waterfarm, Aquafarm or Current Culture Undercurrent single bucket deep water culture system. Such a good system can give you the chance to cut out as many as fifty clones every week from your mother plants. Some other farmers use a large fabric pot that offers so more protection if the pump system should fail. The most important thing regardless of your choice is to pick a system that provides your mother plant with enough nutrients to support its growth.

2) Take your cuttings close to the tip of your mother plant. The idea is to leave a broad, blunt end after the cutting. This will allow your mother plant to receive sufficient illumination to continue growing.

3) On the issue of lighting, it is of vital importance that you keep your mother plant within the glare for at least eighteen hours a day if not the whole day.

4) Be wary of delivering too many nutrients to your mother plant at once. Use nutrients solutions sparingly and if you notice any signs of oversaturation of nutrients, get your mother plant flushed. Also pick off old and dead leaves periodically.

5) Keep relative humidity between 60-65% for your mother plant to survive for long. You can get any portable humidifier to do this for you.

Mother Plant Protection (Against Pests and Diseases)

Since time immemorial, pests have always been the cardinal enemies of plants and cannabis is no exception. These pests and the pathogens they carry around can infect and affect your plant to reduce your yield or even kill off the plant.

Inspecting mother plants for pathogens and pests

Your mother plant or indeed any of your plants are susceptible to attack from certain pests and pathogens. Luckily though, indoor cultivation limits the contact of your plants with these pests. Therefore, it is generally advised to ensure that you do not bring a plant that has been outside into your indoor cannabis garden. This is because it may bear pests and pathogens from outdoors and spread them to your healthy plants.

Let's take a look at some of the more common pests and pathogens starting from fungi. Powdery mildew is the greatest threat possessed by fungi. It is visible on the surface of the leaves where it forms a whitish to grayish layer of powder. Any time you notice such grayish powder, you should get a simple hand lens to inspect. The distinguishing feature is fungal hyphae that rise from the leaf surface. Botrytis is another possible fungal threat especially if humidity levels are too high and you haven't spaced your plants well. These are the two most common pathogens.

Let us talk about pests. Pests are a much more real threat to your plant due to their active presence, highly destructive nature and ability to multiply rapidly within a very short time. The most common pests of cannabis are spider mites, ants, mealybugs, leafhoppers, snails, thrips and root aphids. Spider mites are particularly dangerous to your plant as they can destroy it inside out in less than 72 hours. The key to dealing with these pests is early identification. Therefore, closely examine the mother plant regularly with a handheld lens for signs of changes on the leaves or stem. With a hand lens, you are probably going to get to see and identify the pests themselves. The key is vigilance, awareness and prompt action to save infected plants.

Apart from pests and pathogens, larger animals such as deer and mice may consume your cannabis plant in large quantities. Of course, I do not need to tell you that a deer is more likely to destroy your plant in quick order than insects can. Therefore, you must provide physical barriers against any such animals in your localities. Erecting a fence, or keeping the door to your cannabis room shut are just some of the ways you can defeat these threats.

Controlling pests and parasites

Here we will look at two ways of controlling cannabis pets and parasites

I. *Introducing natural predators*

The organisms listed below may be introduced into the cannabis cultivation environment to battle pets and pathogens. Keep in mind that these are typically useful for outdoor growths.

   a) Amphibians consume snails and slugs.
   b) Aphid midges can help you get rid of many varieties of aphids.
   c) Damsel bugs will solve your thrips, caterpillars, and aphids problem.
   d) Lacewing larvae feed on, thrips, whiteflies, and aphids.

e) Ladybug larvae feast on mites, mealybugs, and aphids.

f) Birds of prey naturally prey on mice. Other birds also feed on insects, even very tiny ones.

g) Wasps kill off caterpillar populations very quickly.

Also, scarecrows and fences can keep way larger animals. You may also consider rodenticides to get rid of rodents.

II.   *Using eco-friendly pesticides*

Pesticides may often be your last resort at avoiding a swarm out due to insects. However, you should be socially responsible enough to use only eco-friendly pesticide solutions. For instance, neem oil is reputed to drive away even the most-stubborn insects. Garlic and onion also drive away a lot of insects due to their repellent odor. Salt is a natural deterrent to most insects. Spraying salt some centimeters away from the base of your plant would also drive away snails and slugs. In any case, though, you can always remove these with your hands when you find them.

Pruning Mother Plants

Mother plants require extreme care if they are to remain vigorous and healthy. Pruning is one of the steps taken to ensure that the mother plant remains in the vegetative state, to provide a reservoir of desired cannabis through clones.

Why prune mother plants?

Many people prune their cannabis plants for various reasons. Pruning refers to the act of taking a large secateurs or scissors to the top end of your cannabis plant and cutting it off. The primary hope is that by pruning, the plant will be encouraged to grow out more lateral stems from the point of pruning. This does follow a certain logic.

Look at the nearest tree close to you. Do you notice the way the main stem starts to branch and subdivide into smaller branches, which then also further divide to create even more branches? The whole aim of the pruning exercise is to generate even more branches and offshoots in the same way. Now, you may ask why more branches are beneficial.

The overarching belief is that more branches mean more leaves and better nutrients available. Most people also prune their plants because they believe this induces the production of more than the one standard bud per plants. Using this method, many growers have successfully induced their plant to produce up to five or more buds.

However, caution must be employed. Not all cannabis strains produce more buds due to pruning or shearing off their tops. Therefore, you must know exactly how the strain you have planted responds to pruning. The only sure thing is that pruning at a 45 degrees' angle will force your plant to develop two new branches growing out from the point of shearing. Other strains may produce more buds but of relatively smaller size. That means the new branches get to share the bud the plant would have produced.

Another reason to prune is for security reasons. Pruning often reduces vertical height for a more even spread of the plant. That can be a deciding factor in deciding whether or not to prune your plant. Pruned mother plants often grow in a compact pattern that sacrifices vertical height for robustness. Growers with sativa plants also use pruning to reduce its size. Without pruning, a sativa plant is likely to possess only one large, main stem that gives off leaves periodically. Leaves would grow only along this stem. This may support its inherent tendency to grow into a very tall plant that may cause issues with privacy and secrecy. Pruning, therefore, can serve as a way of reducing the height of your mother plant and making it look more like a bush than a small tree.

When to prune

People start pruning at very different times in the life cycle of their mother plant. A lot of growers start early by pruning and training clones and seedlings as they grow. However, this can cause adverse effects if too early. It may limit the overall development of the entire plant and cause potential destruction. Instead, you should wait until the shoot system of the plant can withstand the rigors of pruning without compromising the health of the plant. You also have to be mindful of just how much leaves you are losing during your pruning. Your mother plant needs at least 50% of its leaves at all times. If you prune more than this away, the overall viability of your plant is going to be severely indented. A safe bet is to prune around the third week of vegetative growth.

Determining the Sex of the Plant

The sex of a cannabis plant can be determined by what grows between their nodes. The nodes are the notches where branches grow from the main shoot. Of course, the males bear sacs containing pollen while females bear stigmas for pollination. However, you can even identify the sex of a cannabis plant long before the flowering stage by critically examining preflowers with a hand lens. Preflowers emerge in the last stage before actual flowering, but they do so in patterns and structures that indicate what sex the plant is. Look out for the initial development of the sacs in males and the bract that will give rise to the stigma in females. Other methods for early sex determination are available, but none beats looking for the preflowers, in term of ease and accuracy.

Mother plants offer you a surefooted approach to cannabis cultivation. With a mother plant, you can quickly know what traits, in particular, to expect from your growing plants. However, the process of choosing and caring for a mother plant requires due diligence and hands-on attention. Provide this, and you would have saved yourself a world of trouble that might have popped up later on.

CHAPTER 7

HOW TO CLONE CANNABIS PLANTS

What are Clones and Why Use Them?

In cannabis cultivation, a clone refers to a plant that is a replica of another plant. While the words "clones" and "cuttings" may be used interchangeably, it is important to note a slight difference between them. Cuttings refer to the cut-off parts of a mother plant, intended for rooting. Clones, on the other hand, are the already rooted cuttings taken from mother plants.

Cannabis clones are products of asexual propagation of a single, female, mother plant that has been carefully selected and bred for this purpose. Cannabis clones develop from stem cuttings of a mother plant that is replanted to redevelop roots and a shoot system, before growing into a new, healthy plant. With clones, the chances are higher the offsprings are going to have an exact chromosomal copy of the parent. That means a precise DNA material transfer is made and this manifests in the observable traits of clones such as the ability to resist pests and pathogens, and resilience in case of less-than-adequate growth conditions.

The most common type of cannabis clone is created via a plant cutting, but tissue culture is also a viable method used by some commercial researchers.

Why use clones?

There are some reasons why cultivators and home growers alike prefer clones to seeds.

- Cannabis is a heterozygous plant that frequently produces a wide variety of genetic material in offspring during sexual propagation. While this may engender variety, it can also cause unwanted surprises that you will do better to avoid.

- Clones take less time to mature. If time is of the essence, cloning is your best bet. You don't need to wait for your seed to germinate and then sprout. With clones, you are jumping directly into the deep end.

- Clones also save money and prevent uncertainty. It may take more than four weeks to determine the sex of a plant developed from a seed. With clones, however, you can save unnecessary expenses incurred in caring for plants that may grow to become unwanted by you. Imagine wanting a female plant only to discover the seedling you have been tendering for a month is male.

- Clones also give you the chance to experiment and study the effects of varying factors on your cannabis garden. That will give you an edge in subsequent growing seasons.

- Importantly, cloning gives you a chance at a repeat experience. It means you do not have to admire a particular strain once and then, puff; it goes away. No. you can use cloning to preserve the best traits possible in your cannabis for as long as you want.

- Furthermore, cloning helps keep your cannabis farm self-renewing. Usually, a cannabis plant dies off at the end of its flowering cycle. With cloning though, you get to prolong the lifecycle by stopping development at the vegetative stage. This also means that you have the base input for your next farming season. You also get to save cost by not having to spend on seeds next time around.

Increasing Success Rate of Cloning

From our discussion so far, cloning may look quite simple to you. It is simply cut a part of the mother plant, plant in the soil and watch it germinate into an entirely new plant. However, the process can provide some challenges and be difficult to master. The process itself starts from the selection of the right mother plant. If your mother plant is sickly, its clones will inherit that weakness as well. Therefore, you must pay attention and find fortune, to be able to pick an incredible mother plant, one with all the unique characteristics you want and less undesirable traits.

Furthermore, the clones to be replanted aren't always strong. They require tendering and careful attention if they are to survive. If this isn't done, then the chances of a failed cloning process increase.

Here are some other pointers to help you maximize your odds of success in cloning your cannabis plant.

- *Avoid cloning sick plants*

When you have a mother plant, you're excited about, chances are you'd want to clone it. But if it's sick at the moment, you might get confused about what to do. Do you go ahead and try to get a cutting from a clean part of the plant? Yes, you can give that a try but it is risky, and the chances of succeeding are narrowed. While this strategy may work, the odds that such a weakened clone would survive are much dimmer than average. Even if it does survive for a bit, it will need to fight hard to stand a faint chance of surviving. These factors significantly increase the odds of failure. Therefore, it is best and prudent you go for healthy plants instead.

- ***Use sterile instruments for your cuttings.***

Infectious agents abound everywhere, even on the shears that you use to make your cuttings. Therefore, you need to be sure it is sterile before you use it. If you cannot get a new pair of shears for cutting each time, then at the very least, distinguish the shears you use to cut clones from the ones you use to prune other plants.

- ***Stop giving nutrients until you've transplanted your cuttings.***

Hold off on the nutrients until after your transplant is completed. Do not overload the fragile cuttings with nutrients they can't even absorb yet. At the very least, you need to give them a few hours to two days to develop their first roots. If you keep pumping nutrients into the soil when they do not even have the roots to absorb them, then, they may find it hard to thrive when they do eventually get those roots.

Clones vs. Seeds

One of the first things you'll need to decide on when starting to grow cannabis is whether to start from seed or clone. One of the first things you'll need to decide on when starting to grow cannabis is whether to start from seed or clone. Choosing between clones and seeds is without a doubt a landmark decision. I will not attempt to announce a clear winner between clones and seeds; I will rather lay bare the benefits and drawbacks in using either clones or seeds. You can decide based on the variables and plans you have for logistics.

Benefits of using cannabis seeds

- Seeds sprout plants that possess a taproot. Taproots give rigidity and strength to plants.

- Since clones are replicas of their mothers, it can be deduced that they would most likely inherit the bad traits of the mother plants, if any. Using seeds cuts out this possibility, as each is unique in genetic composition and chemical architecture.

- Seeds provide a wider variety of outcomes than clones.

- If for some reason you do procure seeds but don't want to put them to use immediately, you could store them guaranteed that they would still be good by the time you are ready to use them. Seeds have a longer lifespan in contrast to clones, and can usually be stored safely for a long time.

Drawbacks of using seeds

Some of the disadvantages of growing cannabis from seeds include:

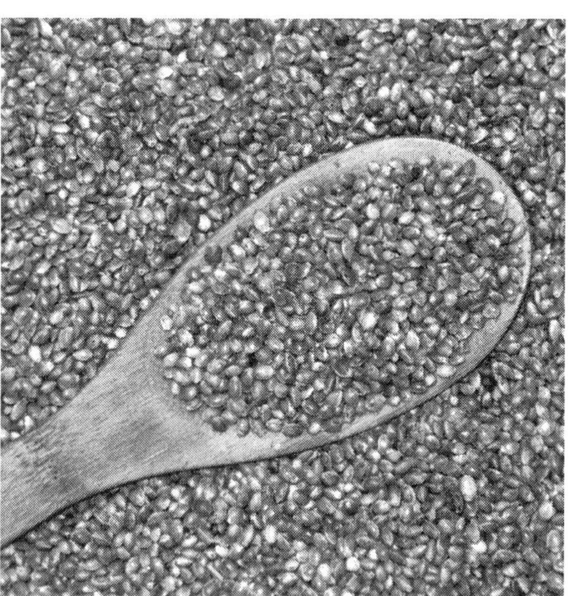

- A grower invests quite a bit of time before they know if the seed is male or female.

- Seeds are very delicate after they pop. It doesn't take much to kill them. This can be a huge issue for new growers who are still just trying to figure things out.
- Germinating seeds is a skill that not everyone possesses. It takes experience to master.

Drawbacks of using clones

Some of the disadvantages of using clones include:

- Clones lack a taproot. Instead, they grow secondary roots also known as a fibrous root system. Many cannabis growers believe that a taproot makes the plant stronger.
- Being replicas of their mother plants, cannabis clones may carry diseases and pests from their mother plants.
- Clones have a limited shelf life. Therefore, you either have to see them through to the end or watch them wither and die.

Basic Steps to Cloning

There are several methods of taking cuttings from your selected mother plant. I will discuss the techniques with the highest success rates in this section. Successful cloning requires the highest standards of cleanliness, and care. Clones are sensitive to their environment. Harsh conditions such too much heat and too much light will increase death rates.

There are several methods of taking cuttings from your selected mother plant. The techniques with the highest success rate will be outlined in this section. Successful cloning requires the highest standards of cleanliness, and care. Clones are sensitive to their environment. Harsh conditions such too much heat and too much light will increase death rates.

Step 1: As I earlier asserted, the most important step in the cloning process is to make a choice of the mother plant to take cuttings from. Once this is done, you are set for work. Get your sharp razor ready (or a pair of scissors, whatever the case might be). As earlier mentioned, using a razor is recommended because they exert lower pressure and are less likely to damage the mother plant. Using the razor, make a clean cut of a branch off the mother plant. The choice of branch should be made considering factors such as health and vigor. Only the healthiest branch(es) should be cut. While making the cut, make sure to cut at an angle, that is, make a diagonal cut of the branch. The cutting angle could be set to anywhere between 40 and 45 degrees, in order to secure a larger surface area for faster rooting. Care must be taken while making the cut to ensure that the mother plant is not damaged in any way. After making the cut, you must immerse the cutting into the water immediately. This should be done for all cuttings.

Step 2: Now, you have your cuttings ready for planting. The next step is to examine your cuttings to make sure they are appropriately structured before proceeding to plant. If there are too many leaves or little branches on your cuttings, you should remove some of the leaves and cut off the little branches, so that your cuttings will fit into the planting medium perfectly. Now, apply the rooting hormone to your cuttings. You must ensure that there are at least 2 to 3 leaves on each cutting above ground level, and 2 sets of trimmed nodes below ground level.

Step 3: Now that the rooting hormone has been applied to your cuttings, dip them into wet, treated grow medium. The setting can be achieved with distilled water. Using an object with a blunt end, make a half inch incision in the growing medium. This allows for root structures to emerge and grow optimally.

Step 4: The next step involves watering the rooting medium. Carefully apply water to the rooting medium until it becomes moist. You must take great care while watering, to ensure that you do not over-water and damage your baby clones' roots. Note that you need to keep your clones moist all the time. You must avoid allowing your clones to get dry at all cost, especially in their infancy. At this young age, conditions must be kept at optimum so as to increase the chances of survival and wellbeing of your clones. You might consider placing them under a humidity dome, in order to keep them moist always and prevent drying.

Step 5: Like other conditions necessary for optimal development of your clones, lighting conditions must be strictly controlled and religiously monitored. It is recommended that you place your clones not more than 24 to 30 centimeters from a fluorescent bulb, while giving them 18 to 24 hours of daily light consumption.

Step 6: Watch your clones fervently for the next few days. Under excellent conditions, roots should begin to develop with 7 to 8 days, and by two weeks, the root architecture should have completely developed. Once this is achieved, you can begin the transplanting process.

Step 7: Examine the root structure of your clones. Clones that have brown, damaged roots should be set aside. Clones exhibiting this sign typically grow very slowly and weakly. However, there have been reports that roots that developed a brown, wilted presentation early on went on to gain strength and grow normally. To this end, roots appearing brownish in color may be allowed 5 to 6 days to restore rigidity. If they fail to normalize after 6 days, then it is advised that clones with such roots are removed from the garden.

Step 8: You may dip your clones into Vitamin B1 before going on to plant them, as this substance is proven to help stimulate root development.

As clones are genetic mirror images of their respective mother plants, the act of cloning allows you to select and maintain certain desirable qualities or characteristics of a mother plant, at relatively low costs.

Cloning is an easier way of growing cannabis, compared to growing from seeds; this means you can all the desirable traits you want while sustaining a high yield. However, if you are new to cloning, the process may not go all smooth and easy the first time, it takes knowledge and experience to master the art of cloning.

CHAPTER 8

CANNABIS GROWING STAGE

Proper Lighting for Cannabis

Cannabis is a kind of plant that thrives under the sunlight. For your cannabis plant to develop into a healthy and quality plant; it will need a minimum of five hours of direct interaction with sunlight but it will grow best when exposed to sunlight the whole day. That also applies to indoor growth.

Therefore, when you are choosing a location to plant your cannabis, pay attention to the amount of light it is likely to receive there. Slopes that face the south get a lot more sunlight than the slopes that face the east and west. This is because western and eastern slopes are usually hidden from the sun during the morning and in the afternoon time, correspondingly. Slopes that face the north are usually cold and they barely get any sunlight.

At higher altitudes, your plant is most likely to be exposed to more sunlight because the atmosphere is delicate and the rate of pollution is lessened the higher you go. The air and the number of impurities at lower altitude intersperse the reflections of the sun. The growers who decide to plant their garden in their backyards often bargain between the requirement for sufficient sunlight and the need to hide their cannabis garden. Just in case there is plant life hanging over or possibly 'looming' over your cannabis field or garden, they should be cut short so that your plants get maximum and direct access to the sun.

There is absolutely no room for shadows over your plants if they must grow well. All other things being equal, a hot climate with lucid, sunny weather will produce a bigger yield of cannabis for you.

Nutrients and Fertilizing Cannabis

Cannabis is a plant which hungers for a sufficient amount of certain nutrients regularly so that it can grow to become big and healthy. We have discussed the majority of these elements in chapter three. During the growth stage, it is especially important that the soil you used to plant your cannabis contains these nutrients or you supplement externally through the use of fertilizers.

Nutrients in the soil will diminish as the plant grows. Therefore, the nutrients must be constantly replenished for the plant to continue to grow actively and healthily. By the time the plant reaches the vegetative stage, your cannabis needs to be fertilized most especially with a fertilizer that has a lot of Nitrogen. The pace at which the plant grows is sometimes restricted because of the field space and the amount of light that reaches the plants. When the plant gets to this stage, in addition to the nutrients in the soil will boost the development and growth. The main aim is to provide the cannabis plants with their nourishing requirements without adding too much fertilizer to avoid the soil from becoming too concentrated.

Bulk fertilizers like rose food can be mixed with the soil to improve yield. As the plants continue to grow, you should remember to never cover up the soil with concentrated or mixed fertilizers, it will allow the growth of molds, diseases and the invasion of pests in your cannabis farm. Bulk fertilizers can also destroy or ruin the plants if they manage to touch the stalk or the root of the plant. During the growth of the plant, nutrients can be fed in liquid form, that is, the nutrients can even be mixed in water for wetting the cannabis plant.

Fertilizers which are capable of dissolving can be natural or chemical and they come in an extensive selection of concentrations and types of nutrients. Examples of natural fertilizers are watery manure and fish oil. Chemical fertilizers usually have nutrients in them; the quantity of each of the three vital elements might be about 20-20-20, or 5-10-5. It could even possibly have only one nutrient, Nitrogen, 16-0-0. As a matter of fact, you can utilize virtually any fertilizer as long as you ensure that the proportion of nitrogen is higher in comparison to potassium and phosphorus.

Generally, the majority of the fertilizers are made for the purpose of utilization at home, however, cannabis is not a home plant. It requires twice the nutrients that home plants require. A practical example of how to fertilize is to fertilize by the fifth week after planting and continuously after that for two weeks till it enters its flowering stage. After that, you can stop the use of the fertilizer except the plants show a strong need or requirement of the fertilizer nutrients.

It is best to fertilize with a solution which is more diluted and needs to be added more times during fertilization than to make use of a very concentrated mix which requires to be added fewer times.

Ensure that your fertilizer has completely dissolved inside water before you spread it on the soil. Remember to use the specified quantity of fertilizer inside a transparent container with a lid, combine it with a glass of water and shake it furiously before allowing it to come to rest. If you figure out that you have issues with the fertilizer dissolving in the water, add some heated water to the mix and shake again. If it does not disintegrate again, make use of a different fertilizer.

Moisten the soil before you decide to fertilize it and you should never add fertilizer to a plant that has no soil. If the soil is dry, first wet it properly with a half quart of water for each cannabis plant. After that, allow the cannabis to stay in its position for about fifteen minutes before fertilizing normally.

Organic Fertilizers

Unlike chemical fertilizers, natural or organic fertilizers have a lesser concentration. Their structure is made up of almost thread-like materials which prepare the soil by boosting its system of water retention. They also increase the content of organic materials in the soil and affect the soil capacity for holding water. Because they are disintegrated by the action of microscopic organisms unlike the chemical fertilizers, their nutrients are given to the soil in soluble fashion. Animal excrement and humus are examples of fertilizers which can be used for virtually every planting purpose. They possess the required nutrients that cannabis requires and can be used for quite a long period of time. Manure which hasn't been composted is very effective but should only be used during the fall season. During winter, the manure composts under the soil layer. Unlike chemical fertilizers, natural fertilizers can be mixed with other forms to provide balanced nutrition.

Chemical Fertilizers

Chemical fertilizers have all the nutrients in a dissolvable form and that allows them to perform their function rapidly. Most times, they are a lot more concentrated than organic fertilizers making them capable of ruining the soil and destroying your cannabis plant when they are used more times than necessary. These kinds of fertilizers come in a wide range of concentrations and proportions of nutrients.

As long as a chemical fertilizer is still packaged, you can see the proportion and ratio of Nitrogen, Phosphorus, and Potassium. You can also find the pH level which shows how much alkalinity or acidity the fertilizer can potentially add to your soil. Chemical fertilizers should not be mixed together because they are often incompatible with each other.

The problem of solubility is also another very big problem with chemical fertilizers because during heavy rainfall or flooding, they will most likely wash away and the only way to solve this problem is to keep applying the fertilizer after rainfall during the period when it is supposed to grow.

Most growers prefer to add fertilizer to the cannabis plant after it has been planted and continuously for six weeks after planting until it commences its flowering stage. Caution should be taken as we earlier discussed to ensure that the fertilizer does not come in contact with the stalk.

FLUSHING CANNABIS PLANTS

Flushing as a process may become important when you over-fertilize your soil and need to get rid of some excess nutrients as a result. The term itself as related to cannabis farming is one term new cannabis farmers might find strange. In flushing your plants, you are basically leaving them to survive on water alone for some time. It is an easy process which may be absolutely vital if you become guilty of over-saturating your plant with nutrients.

When to Flush your Cannabis Plants

To master how to flush the plants, one needs to know when to flush. A few fundamental instances which may necessitate flushing include;

- During the change between nutrition and development cycles

- Lockout of Nutrients

- Before harvesting

Changes in Nutrition

The cannabis plant requires different nutrition supplements throughout its growth cycle. The nutrients it needs vary at different stages of development and growth. For example, the nutrients it requires during flowering are different from what it would need in the vegetative stage. Think of it as cleaning out your bowel in readiness for a fresh meal.

Lockout of Nutrients

A high concentration of nutrients in the soil, inappropriate acid and base levels and other forms of pressure that impact negatively on the growth of your plant may automatically lead to a lockout of nutrients. It could be the accumulation of salt from the nutrients or the acid and base levels that keep absorption from happening which ultimately leads to a reduction in your plants' ability to absorb needed nutrients. Flushing can help you restore the soil to its default setting to deal with this.

When you flush your plants, you get rid of the surplus accumulation of salt and fresh nutrients can then help to repair the pH balance of the soil. Flushing will permit your cannabis plant to continue to soak up nutrients and grow actively at a hearty and favorable pace.

Before Harvesting

The final process of flushing should happen before cannabis is harvested. By doing this, the plant is compelled to use the nutrients it has already reserved during the previous week. If the nutrients aren't used, the impacts may show up negatively in the quality while it is being smoked.

How to Flush Cannabis Plants

As explained before, flushing involves the stoppage of nourishing the plants with food and nutrients and only leaving them to survive on water. To prevent a lockout of nutrients or while you are trying to change the nutrients concentration, you can flush your plants by watering them with a large amount of water that has a pH level somewhere in between 6.0 - 6.8 for soil and 5.5 - 6.5 for hydroponics. Wet the cannabis plant and the soil completely first and repeat after fifteen minutes. This will allow the water to percolate the soil and leach (drain) out any excess nutrient.

To know if the flushing was successful, you can use a TDS reader, TDS stands for Total Dissolved Solids. It can be used to estimate just how clean the water overflow is. If the TDS readings of the water leaking out of your plant pot are the same as or close to the TDS reading of the clean water you are using to flush the plant, then you can be sure that your flushing was successful.

As your cannabis plant continues to grow, lighting remains as important as ever. You will also need to pay attention to the amount of nutrient available for your plant and supplement these with fertilizers if needed. In cases where you have made the nutrients too concentrated, then flushing is an absolute must to prevent your plant from suffering the negative effects.

CHAPTER 9

HARVESTING YOUR CANNABIS PLANT

Harvesting can be referred to as the process of gathering the yield of a plant in one growing season. From personal experience, I happen to know that this is the most enjoyable part of the cultivation of cannabis. From planting the seed, to watching out for the first sprout, through to the process of fertilizing and wetting your plants, nothing gives more joy than the knowledge that you have successfully bred your cannabis plant from mere thought to the beneficial, all-around plant that it is. Let us get down to the business of harvesting your cannabis plant.

Before harvesting, you must understand that the smell of harvesting isn't pleasant and the odor spreads really fast. There is virtually nothing you can do about this except perhaps using a face mask if you are really that offended by the odor.

To know exactly when the time is ripe for you to harvest your cannabis, there are certain signs you must watch out for.

Signs of Harvest in Cannabis Plant

Listed below are some features that help growers know exactly when a plant is ripe for harvest. However, not all of the features exist in all plants which have reached their full growth period.

• *TRICHOME COLOR*

There are several ways to tell exactly when it's the period to harvest your cannabis plant. The most trustworthy method of knowing this however is the trichome color. The trichome is a gland in the plant that brings forth resin and is widely agreed to be the best method to check the maturity of your cannabis. To check the trichome color, you will be required to acquire a magnifying glass as the trichomes are very small.

The trichomes have three chronological color states which are lucid, foggy and amber. Following the color states of the trichomes, the best time to gather your harvest is when part of the trichomes is amber and the other part is either lucid or foggy. The difference in color is due to the fact that the shoots at the top ripen faster than the buds at the lower part. You do not need to hold on for the trichomes to become amber completely as this usually signifies a reduction in the tetrahydrocannabinol and a surge in the amount of Cannabinol.

- ***YELLOW LEAVES***

You can begin to harvest your plants when the leaves start to yellow and you have established this is not due to a deficiency of a nutrient such as magnesium which often affects the pigmentation of deficient plants. When the large leaves of your plant begin to turn yellow or start to drop to the floor on their own, then you can flush the plant in preparation for harvest. However though, as long as you have utilized fertilizers to aid the growth of the plant, then it is highly likely that the leaves will not fall off immediately the cannabis is ripe. This kind of makes the color of the leaves an unreliable factor to know the right time to harvest.

- ***CURLING LEAVES***

When the leaves of your plant begin to curl and dry, that is often a sure pointer to the fact that you need to harvest them. The leaves curl because the cannabis plant reduces its intake of water as it nears its maturity stage. However, before you take this as a definitive call for you to harvest your plant, be sure to check that the curling of the leaves isn't as a result of diseases and pests.

- ***PISTILS***

You can also get to know the time to harvest from examining the effect of light on some of the reproductive parts of the plants. You can examine the ovary, style and stigma to determine whether to start the harvest. When some parts of the pistils are brown, you can begin to harvest your plants.

All the indicators stated above are satisfying indicators to check if the cannabis plant can be harvested but as explained before the most reliable way to check for the maturity of your plant is the trichome color.

It is also important to know that the process of harvesting an Indica is slightly different from a Sativa plant due to the difference in their relative size.

Harvesting an Indica Plant

The plant which will be at most four-foot-long should be cut off at the bottom and should be suspended with the tip of the plant facing downwards inside a chilly room that is dark and has no fresh air. Using a clipper, take out as many of the plant leaves as possible. Then, the subordinate leaves should follow, place the two leaves in different heaps, not together and lastly you should harvest a few trims from the bud. Trims are referred to as the little leaves that are bound with wax or resin.

This way you have about four various qualities of marijuana to select from.

1. The fan leaves will just be an average smoke.
2. The subordinate leaves will have a higher quality than the fan leaves
3. The trim will be quite exceptional
4. The bud is the best part, it has the highest quality and it is the most exceptional

Harvesting a Sativa Plant

This is basically like the process of harvesting the indica plant, only that this requires more labor and effort. Sativa plants are usually grown by those who prefer to grow their plants outdoors. The sativa plants usually grow longer than the indica plant; they can reach up to twelve feet. They cannot be gathered so easily which is why they take a lot more effort.

The sativa plant should be hacked at the base and then arranged on a canvas. Next, the canvas is made into a roll and tied up tightly so that it can be lifted. A canvas sheet per plant is how the sativa plant is transported. Just like the indica plant, the sativa is suspended with the tip facing the ground in a dark room with no fresh air. However, because of the huge size of the plants, you might need to cut the branches individually and suspend them. Using a clipper, take out as many of the plant leaves as possible as in the Indica. Then, the subordinate leaves should follow. Also, harvest a few trims from the bud. Trims are referred to as the little leaves that are bound with wax or resin.

The process of harvesting cannabis is often done in the dark because if the leaves are exposed to light, the tetrahydrocannabinol quantity in the plant reduces.

When is the best time to harvest your cannabis? Early or late?

Harvesting a quality cannabis plant is dependent on time. When you harvest it too early, you will not get any effects of hallucination and when you gather it late you risk the possibility of self-pollination or decaying.

Step by Step Process for Harvesting Cannabis

The method and processes you employ in harvesting your cannabis plants are bound to have an effect on the final grade, effectiveness and quality of the final product. An effective harvest process also means you will get the maximum yield possible for your efforts. The processes involved in harvesting cannabis vary among the plant's gardeners. Due to the size of their cannabis farm, some growers prefer the use of automated machines that can reduce the labor that is required to harvest the plant. However, for a small-scale farmer, it does not really make much financial and logical sense to go this way.

Basically, the entire process of harvesting cannabis involves;

1. The elimination of the fan leaves

2. Trimming or eliminating the leaves close to the flowers

3. Detaching the flowers from the stalk

Apart from all the three steps listed above, other important post-harvest processes are curing, sorting and, drying.

Let's talk about the individual processes.

- ***Fan Leaf Removal***

When you notice the signs that say you can harvest your cannabis, the first thing to do is remove the fan leaves. The fan leaves are often referred to as the large sun leaves. The leaves are seen as the clichéd leaf of cannabis. You can cut them by hand, scissors or a handheld hedge trimmer. Unlike the leaves which are closer to the flower, the large sun leaf does not have as much cannabinoid and most times, cannabis gardeners just get rid of them. After you have removed the fan leaves, you now have two choices. You can wet trim your leaves i.e. trim the leaves in its natural, raw state. Alternatively, you may choose to dry the leaves first, before trimming out the useful part of the leaves.

- ***Drying***

The process of dehydrating the cannabis is performed after the dry or wet trimming process. To dry, the cannabis plant is suspended upside down as a whole or they are cut into smaller branches depending on the size of the leaves.

You should dry your cannabis in a temperature range of sixty-five to seventy-five degrees Fahrenheit and the level of humidity should be between forty-five to fifty-five percent. The drying process must also be done in a dark room because any form of light that comes in contact with the plant could reduce the number of cannabinoids and the unsaturated hydrocarbons in the flowers.

The cannabis plant should be dried within six to seven days and to know if the drying process has been completed successfully, you will notice that the stalk of the plant can be arched and the stalk snaps after bending it.

- **_De-stemming_**

After trimming, the stand of the flowers can be removed and stored in the right container to continue the process of curing. If you decide to use the dry trimming method, it is better for you to start the process of de-stemming after the plants have been dried.

Use a sharp pair of scissors to cut out the stalk of the flowers to detach it from the central stem. Although, the use of automated machines for de-stemming helps to save time and effort, it is not practical for a small-time farmer.

- **_Sorting_**

Sorting helps you arrange your final product in a more efficient way for onwards storage and use. Sorting involves segregating the dried plants into various sizes and allows you to easily pick out whichever part of the cannabis you desire. If you are going to be processing your cannabis in an automated trimming machine, it is easier once all the flowers have been grouped by size. After the cannabis plant has been sorted into sizes, you can then proceed to by a processing machine according to their sizes and the sorting process can also be performed after the plant has been trimmed successfully.

- **_Curing_**

Curing is the final part of the harvest process. The flower is allowed to dry slowly during curing to increase the flavor of its flower. The curing container has to be kept in a cold, dark place. During the first week of curing, the vessels should be opened twice in a day to allow the stored moisture to leave and fresh air to go in. The vessel should be opened less frequently as time goes on. Subsequently, you can open it just once and after a few months, the harvested flower will be of the maximum quality. Properly curing your cannabis can lengthen the quality, taste and the smell of the flowers.

In conclusion, the harvest period is very important in determining the eventual quality of the cannabis you have produced.

CHAPTER 10

HOW TO USE CANNABIS

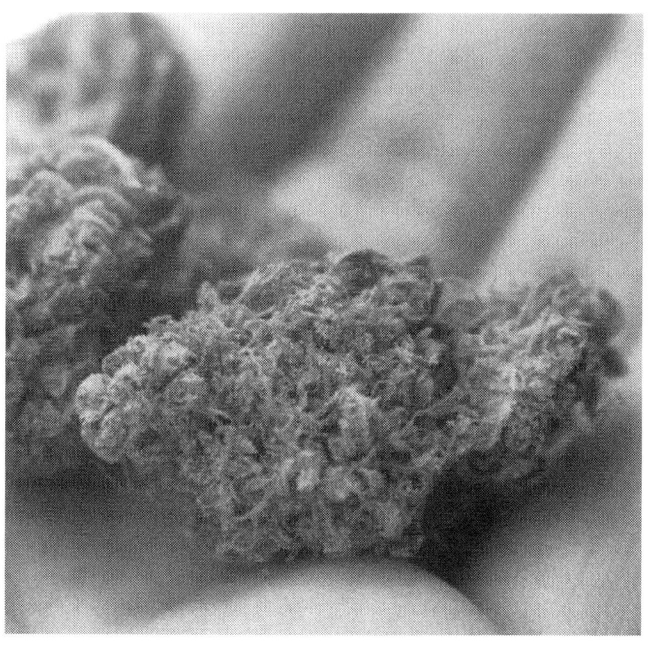

The last chapter in this book delves deep into the many ways you can choose to use cannabis and its products. I have mentioned some basic ways in the first chapter but it is only fitting that we discuss this as a chapter on its own. Surely, the benefits of cannabis outweigh some of the more latent adverse effects. This has prompted its use in various forms and for several ends. Across the world, cannabis is used to cure, improve cognition, create some inner peace and ease, for inspiration, and to improve concentration.

Medically, cannabis has been trialed with ample positive result in the treatment and management of conditions such as Alzheimer's disease, Crohn's disease, several forms of eating disorders (like anorexia nervosa), loss of appetite, muscle spasms, eye diseases like Glaucoma, mental health conditions like post-traumatic stress disorder (PTSD), multiple induration, pains, arthritis, queasiness and cachexia.

There are several ways to take medical cannabis. It can be;

- Smoked
- Eaten as edibles
- Applied as a topical solution to the skin in the form of a cream, cosmetics or an ointment
- Placed beneath the tongue with the help of a dipper
- Consumed as concentrates
- Drunk as a liquid or syrup

There are a lot of other methods available for tapping the benefits of cannabis. Depending on the reason for cannabis use and potential adverse effects, you can select any of them to suit you. The major methods as highlighted above include;

Smoking

Smoking is the most common method of using cannabis and has been around for a very long time. Smoking cannabis can be done in two ways. First, you can smoke cannabis as a joint in which case it is rolled up like a cigarette. In some instances, cigarettes are bought, hollowed out and then the hollow is filled with dried cannabis leaves instead of the usual tobacco. But then, even in instances like this, you can always tell what the person is smoking apart through the scent. Cannabis does not smell like tobacco. The other way of smoking cannabis is through a bong. The content is the same as when rolled up.

The advantage of smoking as a method of using cannabis is that the effects are quickly seen. According to some sources, smoking cannabis may also promote better lung function owing to the deep inhalation involved in the process. This however is debated and that's why I have not included it in the discussion about benefits. Equally, smoking cannabis makes you more prone to the harms discussed earlier. Also, smoking seems to be the most preferred method of use employed when cannabis is being used for recreational and in some cases, spiritual purposes.

Closely related to this method of use is the act of openly burning cannabis as incense. This is usually done for spiritual purposes although it can also be employed for recreational use. It's simple – a user drops cannabis leaves into a burning fire or they constantly feed the fire with these dried leaves. Alternatively, people gather the dried leaves into a heap and set it ablaze. You can guess the result – it's a neighborhood-wide high. As I have mentioned already, there are a number of ways by which you may choose to smoke cannabis. Let us take a closer look at joints, blunts, bongs, bubblers and bowls.

Joints

The joint is the most popular method by which cannabis is taken worldwide due to its ease of preparation and use. You only need the cannabis and the smoking paper to roll it in. There is a variety of smoking paper available, in terms of the various sizes of the paper, and the pulp of wood. The worldwide image of a man smoking cannabis is rolling it up in a paper and lighting up the joint.

Blunts

Just as cigars are to cigarettes, blunts are of similar relationship to joints. Blunts are basically rolls of tobacco that have the tobacco in it taken out and the rolls have been replaced with cannabis. The wrap gives a little more high and a lot of smokers prefer to utilize the alternative flavored cigars which are smaller in size to improve their experience in smoking.

Bongs

Bongs are water tubes that are utilized together with the flower of cannabis and they are preferred by smokers who have a lot more skill. They exist in various sizes and shapes. The water is used to reduce the temperature of the smoke before it gets into your mouth and it allows inhalation to become a quicker process. The water in the bong also serves as a filter to get rid of the cancer-causing substances found in the fumes. The use of bongs makes it efficient to reach a quick and extraordinary high, and it is also a way to simplify large dosage inhalation.

Bowls

Bowls are quite similar to cigarette pipes. They might possibly have the best flavor among all other ways of smoking; they provide a neat hit. Most times, the bowls are created from glass. However, they can also be made from iron, wood, silicone, and ceramics. The bowl serves as a method of using tinier doses of cannabis without adding the smoking film.

Bubblers

Bubblers are like a mix between a water tube and the usual glass pipe. They are a few sizes smaller than the bong and normally a tad bit larger than the normal bowl size. Its method of operation is the same as the bowl, the water cools the smoke before it gets to the mouth and the lungs which gives a perfect hit. It is best for smokers who love to travel with their cannabis and they prefer them in small doses but they still love the water pipes. It is a great choice for novices and intermediate users because it is very simple to use.

Concentrates and Extracts

Concentrates can be referred to as extracts from very active cannabis. They are produced in several forms like wax, hash, resin and amber. The products in this category are not suitable for novices because they are very active and even require specified machinery called a dab rig to be utilized.

Tinctures

Tinctures are described as drops infused with extremely concentrated cannabis. If you do not feel the desire to smoke or if you are in search of an alternative to something edible which has a lesser number of calories, then tinctures are the best choice. Place them under the tongue for quick action and an effect that lasts longer.

Topicals

Topicals are shower products, oils, colognes, basically any product which is used on the surface of the skin. They are usually known to not get the users high, they are non-hallucinogenic. Only a few can get the users high. They are majorly used for the reprieve from critical pain because they contain a large amount of cannabinoid. A practical example of topical use is transdermal patches.

Transdermal Patches

Transdermal patches are applied directly unto the skin and they act similarly to nicotine patches. The transdermal patches have only recently been introduced to the cannabis world. They were made to give relief from pain for those suffering from illnesses which cause serious pains. As soon as the patch is placed on the skin, it supplies a straightforward supply of medical cannabis, giving a considerate and continuous method of relief. You should remember that the patches are not as effective as when the cannabis is being smoked or consumed so it is not advised for users who need an immediate outlet for pain.

Edibles

Eating as a method of using cannabis is another fast-growing trend but it also requires some level of care. It takes a while though for the THC to flow into the bloodstream, because of a slight delay due to digestion. It is a sweetened way of ingesting cannabis but if it is your first time, then you should begin with the smallest measurement possible because it takes a while to figure out the effects of the cannabis.

Eating as a method of using cannabis is also in two major ways. The first is having it as part of the ingredients of processed foods. By this, I mean foods you can buy off the counter in stores. Yes, in countries where cannabis has been legalized, it now forms part of the ingredients used by manufacturers in the production of edible items.

The second way of consuming cannabis by the method of eating is when you add cannabis as an ingredient to your own food. There are countries where it is placed on tables in restaurants as though it is spice. Meanwhile, the oil extracted from the seeds of the plant can also be used for cooking and a common thing made from this is the

Cannabutter which can be used like any other butter for uses such as for baking etc. It could also be the leaves that are ground and used as ingredients in foods such as cakes, cookies etc.

When you are consuming cannabis as part of processed food which you have bought off the counter, be sure to check the label for the quantity that has been used and the dosage that may be required of you. When you are the one adding cannabis to your food from scratch, be careful not to use too much of it. You should bear in mind that eating cannabis directly or indirectly does not produce the effects as quickly as smoking it. You will have to wait for the food to digest and for the nutrients to be absorbed into the bloodstream but you will still get the effects.

Drinking

This is another method of using or taking cannabis and the same rules that apply to eating apply here, too. Do not forget to check the label for details. And if you are the one making the drink yourself, be careful not to use too much quantity. Eating and drinking cannabis are commonly employed as a method of consumption when it is being used for recreational or sometimes medicinal purposes. There are even users who use it to brew tea.

Cannabis Simple Syrup

Cannabis simple syrup is a sweetened liquid produced by a mixture of water and sugar, and saturated with cannabis. It is very simple to make and can be applied to a variety of drinks. It can be produced or created by soaking the flower of cannabis in to create pure syrup; other spices, oils and seasonings could be mixed in with it. Usually, most people who use cannabis simple syrup take it with tea or iced coffee for an exceptional and delicious high.

Other Methods

Aside from these major modes of its usage, cannabis can also be used in the following forms.

Vaporizing

This is the most common method of using cannabis when the purpose is medicinal. But it is also the latest trend even when the purpose is recreational. The advantage of vaporizing cannabis boils down to the health issues surrounding the other methods of using cannabis. In fact, this method is the healthiest and perhaps the most effective way of consuming cannabis, especially for recreational purposes.

When you smoke cannabis as a joint or bong, the leaves burn at about 2000 degrees Fahrenheit. At this temperature, most of the good stuff is destroyed and the remaining stuff is also dangerous. However, with vaporizing, the stuff is not wasted and the consumption is very healthy. Why this is so is readily understood when you understand how the process of vaporizing works.

Heat is also used in vaporizing. However, the process of heating can be conductive or convective. When conductive heating is used, the surface beneath the product is heated to produce the vapor. When on the other hand it is convective heating, the air around the product is heated. Either way, what is produced is way better what is produced when smoking cannabis. More cannabinoids such as THC, CBD and terpenes are produced and carried in the vapors which are then consumed.

THC Bath Soaks

THC bath soaks come in forms similar to bath bombs or salts. It is a simple way of relaxing your body and is quite efficient at reducing the pain of strained tissues and muscles without any hallucinogenic result. You only need to put them in a hot bath and wait to feel the effects after soaking yourself in the water for some time. They are still a very recent method of using cannabis but the few people who have utilized it have found it to be very beneficial.

Pills or Capsules

THC pills which are also referred to as Cannacaps have evolved into a widely known way of using cannabis. The pills contain cannabis which is usually swimming in oil in a capsule. The ingestion of cannacaps is a verified safe method of using cannabinoids for people or users who have problems with their respiratory system. There are quite a number of advantages of using Cannacaps;

- They are usually known to be a lot more harmless than smoking because they provide a uniform and calculable amount of THC
- They give off no smell or fumes unlike when cannabis is being smoked
- They can be mixed with a wide range of other recipes to treat several kinds of illnesses
- It takes a longer period of time before the effects of the THC in it wears off.
- It is easier to incorporate into the dosage of users whose medical prescriptions already include capsules.

Dabbing

These are condensed measurements of cannabis which are gotten by distilling THC and additional cannabinoids. Usually, a solvent like carbon dioxide or butane is used in the distillation. At the end of the process, a gummy oil is produced which most often is referred to as resin, wax, rosin, amber and butane hash oil. Dabbing can turn out to be a complicated method because it requires special pieces of machinery like a dab rig, flashlight, concentrate pen and an array of related equipment to make. However, when it is produced properly, it supplies a neat, great dosage that is not as harsh on the lungs as when cannabis is taken through other methods.

Cannabis for all of its great uses and benefits still offers you so many ways by which you can consume this essentially beneficial herb that has provided succor for men for many millennia. You only need juxtapose your reason for taking cannabis with your comfort and ease of use, and you will be able to select the best option for taking cannabis.

BONUS CHAPTER

MISTAKES TO AVOID WHEN GROWING CANNABIS

In this chapter, I have outlined a number of mistakes commonly made by people who are novices in the art of growing cannabis. To me, these mistakes are sacrilege against the holiness of the plant. And when you make them, the results are usually fatal to your plants or stunt its growth at the very least. I know you are now thoroughly familiar with the process of growing cannabis – you may be familiar with what I am about to discuss here, too, in a way. However, the kind of emphasis to be laid on this will make you realize the importance of the discussion here.

1.   Never Use Unknown Seeds

One thing you must have taken off from the previous chapters in this book is the importance of predictability. In other words, you should be able to have a definite spectrum of expectations from your efforts. This can only be guaranteed when you use familiar premium seeds. If you dabble in the unknown, the results are unknown and disastrous for the enterprise. But you can always take risks if you do not mind the possible attendant loss in effort, time and money.

2.   Never Use just any Soil

No, I am not saying plant your cannabis only in water. I am in fact saying plant it in the soil, but not just any soil, not especially the one in your backyard just because it is there. Choosing the right soil for your babies (cannabis plants) is important because that is the only way they can be born and develop well. In a previous chapter in this book, I have discussed in some details what to look for in the soil to be used.

3. Watch your water

Again, I am not saying you should not use water on your plants at all. I am only saying you should not use just any water. Remember, you need certain nutrients in the water to be used for planting your cannabis. The one from the city can be just too low in the nutrients or just too high. So, do some digging on information available about your water to determine whether your water will be up to the task. Do not forget: cultivating cannabis requires some considerable level of commitment.

4. Avoid too Little Light

Lighting, you know, is important to the survival and robust development of your plant. Cannabis flourishes in the light and this is why you need to ensure your plants get enough light. Be meticulous about this – ensure the source of light is appropriately positioned above the plants.

5. Don't Overfeed or Underfeed Your Plants

We all know what happens when one is underfed – one might get malnourished and even wear the signs on one's skin. When one is overfed, there is a real problem, too. This is the same as your plants. The excitement of starting something new, something tasking, can lead you to overfeed or underfeed your plants. Stick to the feeding schedule and you will be saved from both of these.

6. Mind Your pH Levels

This is the measure of acidity and alkalinity in a substance such as water or soil. This is crucial – it must neither be too low or too high. The standard measure is 7 and you should try as much as possible to stick to this. It is nothing difficult. And if you must adjust the pH level in your soil, do ensure your use natural sources like lime and lemon.

7. Don't be in a Hurry to Harvest

Why are you in a hurry to harvest? If you do not exercise care doing this, you may just render all your efforts up until that moment useless. To get the best quality, you must neither harvest too early nor too late. If you cannot determine when 70% of your buds' hairs have darkened, the right time to harvest, then you should talk to someone more experienced than you are. With time, someone will come to talk to you, too.

8. Don't be in a Hurry to Diagnose

When you notice a deficiency in your plants, do not be in haste to diagnose. You may come up with the wrong diagnosis and ruin the whole of it. The best thing to do though is to talk to someone more experienced. If for one reason or another you cannot talk to someone, then take some good time out to do your research before you conclude on what to do next.

9. What about your Electricals?

Safety, your safety, is very important. While your plants need water, heat and lighting, you need to live and remain in good health in order to literally and figuratively enjoy the fruits of your labor. To this end, you need to take all necessary precautions when working in your garden. Water is a good conductor of electricity so avoid their contact and do avoid your contact with the two, too. You should not mind the money – take the precaution. The best way to go about this is to have a good electrical plan and follow it through.

10. Ask if You Don't Know

Not knowing is not a crime and it is not a crime to ask if you do not know, too. Do not be shy! Do not be afraid to seek help when you are out of ideas or when you are unsure of what to do. Practice makes perfect. Again, someone will soon come seeking your help, too, soon.

CONCLUSION

There you have it. The preceding eleven chapters have been tailored to help you find solutions to the myriad of problems that you may encounter in your quest to grow cannabis for your personal use. Given the relatively *dangerous* nature of trying to purchase cannabis for personal consumption in most territories of the world, it makes a lot of sense for you to learn to grow the little quantity you may probably need.

As I am sure you have realized by now, cannabis is a fairly easy plant to grow. The processes involved may be varied but generally, they are easy to follow. Taking care of your cannabis may take a bit more time and effort especially in the beginning before your plants get into the vegetative phase. However, as long as you keep up the right lighting, temperature and a good supply of nutrients for your plants, you can barely go wrong. Do remember to watch out for pests as well.

Half of the successes and failure in trying to grow personal cannabis is down to the wrong choices of the system. That is why you need to be extra diligent in choosing your soil type, lighting, seed and deciding where to grow your cannabis. Most times, once you get your initial system right, your plant itself takes up the battle to ensure you have a great harvest and a good, steady yield of cannabis is guaranteed. I do hope the information in this book helps you with that and the other processes required to become a successful cannabis grower.

The Holy Grass, cannabis does not deserve to be called "weed" or treated like one. Rather, cannabis, a cure for many an ailment, a popular amongst shrubs, the inducer of ecstasy, of ingenuity and of creativity, deserves a place of honor among the plants we grow. Less dangerous than cigarettes, not as intoxicating as alcohol, less addictive than your everyday coffee, self-sustaining and resilient as a plant, why exactly should you not consume, or grow the cannabis you plan to consume? Absolutely no reason!!!

Good luck growing your cannabis!!!

CANNABIS COOKBOOK

Quick and Simple Medical Marijuana Edible Recipes

BY JOSEPH BOSNER

© Copyright 2019 - All rights reserved.

The content contained within this book may not be reproduced, duplicated or transmitted without direct written permission from the author or the publisher.

Under no circumstances will any blame or legal responsibility be held against the publisher, or author, for any damages, reparation, or monetary loss due to the information contained within this book. Either directly or indirectly.

Legal Notice:

This book is copyright protected. This book is only for personal use. You cannot amend, distribute, sell, use, quote or paraphrase any part, or the content within this book, without the consent of the author or publisher.

Disclaimer Notice:

Please note the information contained within this document is for educational and entertainment purposes only. All effort has been executed to present accurate, up to date, and reliable, complete information. No warranties of any kind are declared or implied. Readers acknowledge that the author is not engaging in the rendering of legal, financial, medical or professional advice. The content within this book has been derived from various sources. Please consult a licensed professional before attempting any techniques outlined in this book.

By reading this document, the reader agrees that under no circumstances is the author responsible for any losses, direct or indirect, which are incurred as a result of the use of information contained within this document, including, but not limited to, —

errors, omissions, or inaccuracies.

INTRODUCTION

I want to thank you for choosing this book, *Cannabis Cookbook – Quick and Simple Medical Marijuana Edible Recipes,* and hope you find the book helpful in gathering all the information you need to understand cannabis and how it can be used in cooking.

There are different ways in which you can consume cannabis, and the most popular form is cannabis edibles. Yes, you can cook with cannabis! It is quite easy to cook with cannabis, provided you are armed with the appropriate information. If you want to learn how to cook with cannabis, then this is the right book for you. This is a detailed guide on cooking with one of the most popular ingredients—cannabis! Before you get started, there are a couple of things that you must know. For instance, what is the ideal personal dosage, and how can you measure the potency of cannabis? What are the common mistakes that beginners make while cooking with it and the ways you can avoid them? Well, if you want to learn about all this, along with other things, then you have chosen the right book.

In this book, you will learn about cannabis edibles, the health benefits they offer, the things to keep in mind while buying and cooking with cannabis, and the different tips you can use to troubleshoot any issues while cooking with cannabis. Apart from all this, you will find various recipes to cook cannabis edibles. The recipes given in this book are quite simple and easy to understand. You merely need to gather all the ingredients that you need, follow the recipes, and voila! Within no time you will be able to start cooking cannabis edibles quite easily!

So, let us get started without any further ado!

CHAPTER ONE

ABOUT CANNABIS

Cannabis, marijuana, or weed, regardless of the name, has quite a long history of human usage. Evidence shows that most ancient civilizations used to cultivate the cannabis plant for the various medicinal benefits it offers. The cultivation of this plant can be dated back to around 500 BC in Asia. The history of cannabis use in the western regions dates back to the early colonists in America, who used to grow hemp plants for making textiles and ropes. The hemp plant was originally cultivated in the regions of Central Asia before it was brought to Africa, Europe, and the Americas. Hemp plants not only grow quickly, but they have different uses as well, and this is the reason why cannabis was widely cultivated in the regions of colonial America and the Spanish missions. The early strains of the hemp plants had a low level of tetrahydrocannabinol (THC). Some evidence also suggests that the cultivators were aware of the psychoactive properties of the hemp plant.

There are various strains of the cannabis plant, and they can be widely classified as cannabis indica, cannabis sativa, and cannabis ruderalis. The popular use of cannabis as a recreational drug because of the high levels of THC found in some strains is the reason why there are strict rules about its cultivation. However, it doesn't mean that cannabis doesn't have any health benefits. In fact, the use of cannabis for medical purposes has become quite popular, and it has been legalized in different countries.

Sir William Brooke O'Shaughnessy, an Irish doctor who was studying in India during the 1830s, discovered that extracts of the marijuana plant could be used to reduce pain and nausea in those suffering from cholera. By the late 1800s, cannabis extracts were sold in doctors' clinics and pharmacies throughout the USA and Europe for treating stomach ailments and other problems. Different studies that were conducted later showed that the compound THC is responsible for the different benefits marijuana offers. Not just the medicinal benefits, but also the psychoactive effects of marijuana are caused because of THC.

The widespread use of cannabis as a recreational drug was rather alarming, and this led to its prohibition by the government. In fact, the Controlled Substances Act of 1970, enacted under President Richard Nixon, prohibited the use of cannabis. Once people started to realize the various medicinal benefits that cannabis offers, there was pressure from different groups to legalize the use and cultivation of marijuana. Cannabis can be used to alleviate the unbearable and painful symptoms of different chronic ailments like cancer, arthritis, and so on. The growing popularity of cannabis as a substitute for pharmaceutical painkillers led to the introduction of different reforms for the legalization of cannabis within the US for medical purposes. In fact, the first state to legalize the use of cannabis for medical purposes was California. Since 2018, medical marijuana has been legalized in a lot of states in the US. However, the laws about the legalization of marijuana keep changing, and therefore, I suggest that you always go through the laws of your state before you start using marijuana in any form.

The two different types of cannabinoids that are naturally present in the resin of the marijuana plant (cannabis sativa) are tetrahydrocannabinol (referred to as THC) and cannabidiol (CBD). These substances tend to react with the cannabinoid receptors present in the body. However, there are different effects that are brought about by these components. This is the reason why CBD is preferred in medical treatment over THC.

Difference between THC and CBD

What exactly is THC?

The main psychoactive ingredient present in the marijuana plant is referred to as THC. This is the agent that is primarily responsible for creating the feeling of being "high" that is associated with the use of marijuana. This compound works by replicating the effects of anandamide. Anandamide is a neurotransmitter that is produced naturally in the human body and it helps to modulate sleeping and eating habits as well as the perception of pain by the mind.

The main effects of THC include feelings of relaxation, altered senses (smell, sight, and hearing), fatigue, hunger, and reduced aggression.

The medical applications of THC

Research conducted for understanding the medical applications of THC show that it might be useful in:

- Reducing the various side effects of chemotherapy, like nausea and vomiting, along with improving appetite

- Helping treat multiple sclerosis by easing painful spasms while improving bladder function

- Helping to relieve pressure in the eyes of people with glaucoma

- Alleviating certain symptoms of AIDS by increasing appetite

- Reducing tremors experienced in cases of spinal injury.

What is CBD?

The chemical formulas of THC and CBD are the same. However, the atoms are arranged differently in CBD. This slight variation is what enables THC to create a psychoactive effect, whereas CBD doesn't do this. About 40 percent of cannabis extract is constituted of CBD. There is plenty of it that's available in nature, and this, coupled with the fact that it doesn't make the user "high," makes it a good candidate for medical use.

The main effects of CBD include the reduction of psychotic symptoms, reduction in levels of anxiety, reduction in inflammation, and relief from convulsions as well as nausea.

The medical applications of CBD

Research shows that CBD can be quite helpful to reduce the psychotic symptoms caused due to schizophrenia and helps manage social anxiety disorder by reducing the levels of anxiety. It can be successfully used for treating depression by decreasing depressive symptoms in an individual. It can also be used for managing the side effects of cancer treatments by stimulating appetite and reducing pain and nausea.

CBD
oil

CHAPTER TWO

ABOUT CANNABIS EDIBLES

What are cannabis edibles? Food that is infused with cannabinoids is referred to as a cannabis edible. Edibles come in different forms like brownies, cookie dough, and so on. It is a popular notion that cannabis can only be added to sweet treats. Well, this might be a popular notion, but it is nothing more than a misconception. You can use cannabis-infused oil or butter in any recipe that calls for regular oil or butter. So, any food, regardless of whether it is sweet or savory, that is infused with cannabinoids is referred to as an edible.

There are different forms in which cannabis edibles are available. Cannabis edibles can be made in the form of brownies, candies, chocolates, cookies, drinks, popcorn, and so on. You will find various recipes for cannabis edibles in this book. Edibles don't have to be restricted to desserts and can be in the form of savory items too. A lot of readily available cannabis edibles look like regular foods. So, you need to carefully go through the labels of the products you purchase. Also, you need to store edibles in a cold and dark place without any moisture. Please store the cannabis edibles such that they are out of the reach of children and pets.

You might be wondering if cannabis edibles have the same effect as smoking edibles. This is a common concern. To put it simply, the effect of consuming edibles is quite different from smoking cannabis. In fact, when you smoke cannabis, it has an instantaneous effect, while cannabis edibles can take a while to start working. It usually takes about 30 minutes to up to two hours for cannabis edibles to take effect. Also, the effects of cannabis edibles usually last longer than smoking.

Another question that a lot of people have is why cannabis edibles seem to have a stronger effect. The quantity of THC present in cannabis edibles is quite varied. This is one reason why it becomes rather difficult to keep track of the amount of THC a user consumes. The THC content in homemade cannabis edibles tends to be quite varied. A lot of users are caught unawares by the potency and long-lasting effects that edibles have.

So, who can buy cannabis edibles? Different states have different rules about the purchase and legality of cannabis edibles. There isn't a uniform law about the legality of cannabis, at least not yet. For instance, medical, as well as retail cannabis is legalized in Colorado. In Denver, any individual who is at least 21 years old can legally purchase and use retail cannabis. Before you start using cannabis in any form, please ensure that its use is legalized in the state that you live in. After all, ignorance of the law is not a defense! The use of cannabis is not advisable for pregnant women and minors.

Edibles are also known as medibles, and these items usually contain THC. Activated cannabis refers to oils or plant materials whose psychoactive properties are heat-activated. These psychoactive substances are the reason why a person experiences a "high" after consuming cannabis edibles. Edible cannabis treats have been used by humans for hundreds of years. In fact, in some places in Eastern Europe, a popular form of medicine was candies infused with cannabis. Also, in India, a drink made with cannabis, known as bhang, is quite popular. The history of this drink dates back to around 2000 BC. Bhang is made with psychoactive cannabis and has been used for a long time for spiritual and medicinal reasons. In western countries, cannabis is usually infused into a variety of treats and isn't limited to just a couple of items.

Cannabis edibles are quite different from all the other forms of cannabis that are available. Cannabis edibles are preferred over other means because their effects last for longer. Ingesting cannabis gives a different experience than inhaling it. Edibles are stronger, and the psychoactive high that they give is more potent. The potency of cannabis edibles can come as a pleasant surprise to even regular users of cannabis.

So, how long does it take for edibles to produce the desired effect? If you are inhaling cannabis, then you can experience its psychoactive effects within no time. However, edibles need a while longer. The amount of time before cannabis edibles take effect will vary from one individual to another. This is the reason why it is important to get the dosage of THC in cannabis right. The metabolic rate of your body, whether you are consuming cannabis after a meal or 0n empty stomach, along with several other factors, influences the time that edibles need to take effect. Since it takes a long time for its activation, it is advisable that you give your body at least an hour or two before you increase the dosage of the edibles. Once you realize the way cannabis affects your body, you can start increasing or decreasing the dosage of cannabis accordingly.

Edibles not only take a while to take effect, but their effect also tends to last for up to six to seven hours if the right dosage has been administered. If you consume a rather large amount of cannabis edibles, then the effects of cannabis might still be felt for up to 24 hours. A high dosage of cannabis means that on the following day you might experience lethargy, mild headaches, and even some fatigue. If you feel like your motor skills have slowed down slightly, that's also a potential side effect of the residual cannabis in your system and will wane in a couple of hours.

Why are edibles considered to be more potent than the other forms of marijuana? To put it simply, this is because edibles are metabolized by the body and this makes them more potent. When you smoke or inhale cannabis, then the psychoactive ingredient in cannabis, THC, is absorbed by the lungs, and from there it enters the bloodstream. Once it enters the bloodstream, it is transported to fatty tissues present in the body like the brain, wherein the psychoactive ingredient connects with the receptors present in the cells.

However, when you eat cannabis edibles, then the edibles need to be digested in the stomach and the intestinal tract. Apart from this, the edibles also need to be metabolized by the different enzymes in the liver before you can start experiencing the effects of consuming cannabis edibles. The enzymes present in the liver will start breaking down the THC present in cannabis. When THC is synthesized in this manner, the resultant product is 11-hydroxy-THC. This compound is more potent than THC. The 11-hydroxy-THC is smaller than THC and enters brain cells more easily than regular THC. All this takes some time and therefore, cannabis edibles take a while longer to take effect than other forms of cannabis.

Another question that worries cannabis users is whether one can overdose on edibles. Well, it is not likely that one can have a fatal overdose by consuming cannabis. However, this doesn't mean that there are no side effects of consuming large dosages of cannabis. Consuming large quantities of cannabis might lead to the user experiencing discomfort for a couple of hours. Some negative side effects of consuming cannabis include paranoia, drowsiness, red eyes, dryness of the mouth, and anxiety. You will learn more about the short-term and long-term side effects of consuming cannabis in the coming chapters. The only thing that you can do if you have accidentally consumed a large dosage of cannabis edibles is to wait it out. You need to sit tight and wait for the symptoms to fade away.

There are a couple of things that you can do to counteract an intense high that you might experience if the dosage of cannabis edibles is high. You can try distracting yourself by listening to relaxing music or even by sleeping. Experts also suggest that chewing on fresh peppercorns can help to ease some of the anxiety that THC induces. Apart from this, you can also try taking some CBD to counteract the THC in your system. Instead of doing all this, I suggest that you start with a small dosage, especially if you have never consumed cannabis edibles before. Always listen to your body when you are using cannabis in any form.

It might happen that you don't feel any of the effects of cannabis edibles that you consume. Do you know why this happens? This might be due to something referred to as first-pass metabolism. At times the enzymes present in the liver start cleaning out compounds that they deem to be unnecessary and in this process, the enzymes might get rid of the THC as well. Instead of metabolizing the THC, this compound is altogether eliminated from the body. The first-pass metabolism can reduce or even completely eliminate the effects of cannabis. In fact, this is the reason why some people tend to need a higher dosage of cannabis than others. To counteract this mechanism, please ensure that you eat something before consuming the cannabis edibles. In fact, it is a good idea to have a fatty meal so that the THC can be easily metabolized. THC is fat- soluble and if you have some fat readily available in your system, it will be easier for your body to metabolize the THC from the cannabis you ingest. You must always wait for at least two hours to allow the THC in the cannabis to be activated. So, even if you don't feel like the cannabis is working, wait for at least two hours before you consume some more.

Purchasing Cannabis

Before you can start cooking cannabis edibles at home, there is another important step that you must not skip. Are you wondering what this step is? Well, you do need to buy the plant material before you can start cooking, don't you?

So the first thing that you must ensure is that cannabis has been legalized in your state. If you happen to reside in a state where legal cannabis is available, then you can get started. In this section, you will learn about where you can buy legal cannabis.

The first thing that you need to do is find a cannabis dispensary! For purchasing cannabis, you need to be at least 21 years old and must have a valid ID. A quick Google search will help you find all the legal cannabis dispensaries within your neighborhood. You can also use several online store locator tools for finding cannabis dispensaries. You can also check the online reviews of the dispensaries! You can explore a couple of different shops since each dispensary will have different products available. Once you find a dispensary that you are happy with, the next thing you ought to do is learn about the cannabis basics. You can always ask the staff at the dispensary for suggestions, but I suggest that you do a little research by yourself. So take some time out of your schedule and read about the different strains of cannabis and the recommended dosage of THC that you need. By doing this basic research, you will be able to make an informed decision.

Once you do all this, it is time to pick up the cannabis item that you need. You can purchase cannabis flowers, readymade edibles, concentrates, pre-rolls, and even other types of cannabis body products.

Now that you know what cannabis edibles are and the ways in which you can buy them, the next question that you might be wondering about is the cost of cannabis edibles! Edibles can be a rather cost-effective means of consuming cannabis, but all this depends on your level of tolerance as well as the options that are available at the local dispensary. The cost of one gram of cannabis flowers can be as high as $20 per gram, and this depends on the area where you live. The cost of edibles primarily depends on the kind of product you are purchasing and the type of edible you want to buy. At times, dispensaries have sales on specific products. As with any other food item, the cost of readymade cannabis edibles depends on the ingredients that are used, along with the type of cannabis that has been used. The cheapest available option for cannabis edibles is cannabis-infused caramels that can cost anywhere between $1 and $3.

CHAPTER THREE

ALL ABOUT CBD

What is cannabidiol? Cannabidiol or CBD is a natural substance found in the cannabis plant that has recently attracted attention for various reasons. Cannabidiol is a relatively new discovery and therefore has still not been thoroughly researched. The results gathered so far from all the research are rather promising. However, there is a lot of misinformation around this topic. The popularity of CBD oil is definitely growing, as is its use.

Since the use of CBD oil is relatively new, there are still some loopholes in terms of impact. In this section, you will learn the basics of cannabidiol.

Where does the CBD come from? Hemp is a specific strain of cannabis and is used to extract cannabidiol. The cannabis plant contains about 85 different types of cannabinoids and CBD is one of them. CBD is the second most common compound in hemp and makes up about 40 percent of extracts. This is where all the confusion starts.

Another common ingredient in cannabis is THC. THC is an intoxicating compound and is responsible for the "high" that users experience. There is a lot of stigma associated with using CBD. This stigma is the result of the simple fact that people consider CBD THC. All these concerns are unfounded, but to some extent understandable, especially since all the terminology used in connection with the CBD may be very confusing.

Here are a couple of terms that you must be familiar with while dealing with cannabis.

Cannabis

It is a flowering plant. The three different types of cannabis are ruderalis, indica, and sativa. Cannabis not only has medicinal applications, but industrial ones too. Cannabis has been used for ages for its tough fiber, oils, and other medicinal uses. However, it is also a very popular recreational drug and therefore the cultivation of marijuana is strictly regulated since some strains of cannabis tend to have high levels of THC.

Hemp

It is a commonly available variety of cannabis and is solely used for its fiber, seeds, and oils. Hemp can be transformed into a variety of products like wax, cloth, pulp, resin, paper, rope, oil, and even fuel.

Cannabinoids

This term refers to naturally and artificially created chemical substances. There are various cannabinoids and they all have different effects—there are some that have a calming and a relaxing effect whereas the rest are categorized as illegal drugs.

CBD

CBD is a naturally occurring chemical in a cannabis plant and is the second most abundantly available constituent of a marijuana plant.

CBD is legalized and is safe for consumption but is still confused with THC.

THC

The most abundant component of a marijuana plant is THC, a psychoactive cannabinoid. This is responsible for the high that the users experience when smoking cannabis and therefore, the use and production of THC are strictly regulated.

Psychoactive

If a chemical compound can directly affect the central nervous system, then it is said to be psychoactive. There are various medical uses for psychoactive substances. In fact, they are used in anesthetics, psychiatric drugs, and so on, but some of these substances are purely used for recreational purposes, can have a variety of side effects, and are highly addictive.

It is a common misconception that CBD oil can make a user experience the feeling of being "high." This is nothing but a misunderstanding. CBD is not psychoactive and does not affect your mental functions. In other words, CBD can in no way have any sort of effect on your mental functions, so you will not feel high or like you are stoned even when you consume a lot of CBD-oil-infused products.

You might be wondering why this happens. Well, only cannabis plants grown specifically for high levels of THC will make you feel like you are high. However, not all cannabis plants are the same, and there are other cannabinoids in the plant besides THC. Some plants are bred solely because of the high amount of CBD and are known as hemp. Hemp plants have only traces of THC (less than 0.3 percent). The combination of high levels of CBD in combination with nonexistent levels of THC does not make CBD products derived from cannabis psychoactive.

Now, you may wonder, if CBD does not make you high, then what does it do? Without going into depth about the different technical aspects of the way CBD functions, here is a brief explanation of what CBD does. CBD affects several receptors in your body, instead of directly binding your cannabinoid receptors such as THC; CBD has an indirect effect on these receptors and increases the number of endocannabinoids produced in the body. This causes the user to feel relaxed when CBD oil products are ingested or vaped. When CBD-based products are used topically, the pain, swelling, or discomfort in a particular area are reduced. The effects of CBD are quite mild and are limited to impacting unpleasant symptoms that torment you, without interfering with your daily life.

Many CBD users worry that even after 30 minutes of using CBD oil, they will not feel differently and wonder if it works or not. Well, give CBD an hour, and you will almost forget all about any sort of discomfort that you were previously experiencing. With CBD, you will not feel like you are high. All it does is relieve pain.

CBD is used to relieve pain, anxiety, and is also at times used in lieu of a sleeping pill. So, is CBD a drug or not? Yes, CBD is cannabinoid. Is CBD found in drug tests? Even if it is used for the right reasons, any drug that shows up in a drug test does not spell good news.

To answer your question, it is very unlikely that any traces of CBD will appear in a drug test. Most of the drug tests that are administered are designed to pick up any trace amounts of THC and not CBD. CBD is a chemical substance, and as soon as you take it, it is broken down by your body. The average drug test is not so complicated that, unlike THC, it can detect traces of CBD. CBD is chemically different from THC, and no pure CBD is detected. However, most cannabis-derived CBD products usually contain traces of THC.

Even if the CBD oil contains only a small amount of THC, will you pass a drug test? There are several types of drug tests, each with different detection thresholds. Even if your CBD oil contains traces of THC, this is impossible to prove in a drug test. There is no standardized test for CBD, and a special test is required. So, if you are worried about any upcoming drug tests at your workplace, you don't have to worry. The employer must specifically designate a test that can detect CBD. All this is just an extra cost for the employer. Since CBD is not psychoactive, it does not adversely affect the body's nervous or musculoskeletal system. Thus, you do not need to worry about CBD negatively affecting your life.

The legality of CBD oil is a rather complex subject. With the increasing efforts to legalize medical marijuana, it is important to understand which aspects of cannabis are and are not legalized.

In the US, nine states have legalized the use of marijuana for recreational purposes. The main reason for the legalization of the CBD, one of the cannabinoids, is that it has several therapeutic purposes. The most popular form of CBD is CBD oil. It is a combination of CBD extract and carrier, such as coconut oil, that can be swallowed or evaporated. Legalizing marijuana is a rather dismal topic where you have to deal with federal and state laws. The legality of CBD oil can be complex. Let's look at the legality of the CBD oil.

Is CBD oil legal at the federal level? Although many states have legalized various forms of marijuana, the US Drug Enforcement Administration (DEA) still classifies CBD as a Schedule I though it has now been approved for medical use

The legalization of marijuana is going through a rather complicated transitional phase, and there are also a few exceptions. The US Food and Drug Administration recently approved Epidiolex, which is used to treat rare conditions of epilepsy and contains CBD. The DEA has classified this as a Schedule 5 drug, indicating a low propensity for addiction and abuse.

The 2014 Farm Bill is often used by cannabis producers selling CBD products to legalize their activities. This law provides for the legal cultivation of cannabis if it is used for agricultural research or for another state pilot program. However, there is still some confusion as to whether the legalization of cultivation involves selling the crop or not. There is no clear definition of the legality of the CBD at the federal level. Therefore, it is a good idea to go through state laws to determine the legality of the CBD oil in a particular state.

Which States Allow Oil Production In The CBD?

Currently, CBD oil is fully legalized in Idaho, Nebraska, and South Dakota. Each state has its own specifications for the legal use of cannabis.

In ten states in the United States, the use of marijuana for medical and recreational purposes is fully legalized. The list of states includes Alaska, California, Maine, Colorado, Massachusetts, Oregon, Michigan, Washington, Vermont, and Nevada. If you are 18 or older, you can legally buy CBD oil at a pharmacy. Medical marijuana is approved in several other states, including Arizona, Florida, Connecticut, Arkansas, Illinois, Delaware, Hawaii, Missouri, New Jersey, Louisiana, New York, Minnesota, Montana, New Jersey, Maryland, North Dakota, Ohio, New Hampshire, Ohio, West Virginia, Rhode Island, Oklahoma, Utah, and Pennsylvania.

Cannabis is legal in about 33 states in one form or another. There are certain states in which the use of CBD oil is medically acceptable, and these are Alabama, Georgia, Indiana, Iowa, Kansas, Kentucky, Mississippi, North Carolina, South Carolina, Texas, Tennessee, Virginia, Wyoming, and Wisconsin.

In 2018, the Senate introduced a new version of the law on farms to update the previous bill. An important part of this bill is that hemp will be legalized at the federal level if the bill is adopted. If and when hemp is legalized, this is a big step forward for the CBD industry, since CBD oil is extracted from hemp.

CHAPTER FOUR

BENEFITS OF CANNABIS

The use of marijuana for recreational purposes steadily grew from 1850- 1930. With the increase in the use of this drug, the government decided to classify cannabis as a Schedule I drug under the Controlled Substances Act of 1970. This led to an increase in the controversies that surrounded the medicinal benefits that cannabis offers. THC finally received the approval of the US Food and Drug Administration in 1985. The US government also sponsored a study in 1999 into the benefits of cannabis and how it helps certain conditions. This study was undertaken by the Institute of Medicine and showed that cannabis helps reduce the side effects brought about by chemotherapy. Since 1999, there have been various studies directed at proving the health benefits that cannabis offers. In fact, California was the first state to legalize the use of medical marijuana in 1966 and since then several states have legalized the use and distribution of medical marijuana.

In this section, you will learn about the various health benefits that cannabis offers.

Slows Down Cancer

A study that was published in the *Journal of Molecular Cancer Therapeutics* claimed that cannabidiol from cannabis is capable of stopping the spread of cancer by disabling a gene known as Id-1. In 2007, the researchers at the California Pacific Medical Center, San Francisco, discovered that CBD could also assist in preventing the cancer cells from spreading. The study that led them to this conclusion was based on experiments on breast cancer cells that have a rather high level of Id-1 and the researchers treated this with cannabidiol. This study showed optimistic results since the addition of CBD helped decrease the mutation of the Id-1 and also slowed the growth of the cancerous cells. Now it is believed that cannabis can help slow the growth of tumors in the brain, breasts, and even lungs.

Prevention of Alzheimer's

In a study[1] that was conducted by Kim Janda from the Scripps Research Institute in 2006, it was observed that THC could help to slow the progress of Alzheimer's. In this study, it was discovered that THC could help to slow the development of amyloid plaques by preventing the enzyme present in the brain, which synthesizes them. This harmful plaque tends to destroy brain cells and increases the risk of Alzheimer's. Controlling the development of these plaque cells helps prevent Alzheimer's.

Treating Glaucoma

Cannabis can be used in the treatment of glaucoma. Glaucoma is a severe problem where there is an increase in the pressure in the eye that can lead to the loss of vision and severe damage to the optic nerves. Several studies undertaken by the National Eye Institute have showed that cannabis can help to reduce the pressure within the eye and this, in turn, can help in the treatment of glaucoma.

---

[1] News Release | Scripps Research. (2019). Retrieved from
https://www.scripps.edu/news-and-events/press-room/2006/080906.html

Reducing Arthritis

A study that was conducted in 2011 showed that cannabis could be used for reducing pain and inflammation that is associated with arthritis. The study also showed that it could help those suffering from rheumatoid arthritis get better sleep while reducing the pain and discomfort that they might experience due to their painful condition. The researchers present in various rheumatological departments in different hospitals started administering Sativex (a pain killer based on CBD) to their patients and within two weeks, the users of Sativex reported a reduction in their pain and an improvement in their ability to sleep.

Epileptic Seizures

A study conducted in 2003 showed that cannabis could help to control epileptic seizures. Robert J DeLorenzo, at the Virginia Commonwealth University, administered cannabis extracts as well as synthetic cannabis to epileptic rats and this helped in stopping seizures in the test subjects within ten hours. Further research suggests that THC can help to control seizures by stabilizing those brain cells that influence the excitability and regulate relaxation

Cannabis can help reduce certain neurological effects as well as the muscle spasms that painful conditions like multiple sclerosis can cause. A study published by the Canadian Medical Association showed that cannabis could be helpful in easing the pain that multiple sclerosis causes. In a clinical study that was conducted by Jody Cory Bloom, it was shown that cannabis could help significantly reduce the pain that these patients experience. The study consisted of 30 patients suffering from multiple sclerosis who weren't responding to any other pharmaceutical drugs. It was observed that by smoking cannabis for a couple of days, the pain that these individuals experienced was reduced. The THC present in cannabis binds itself with certain receptors present in nerves and muscles and this, in turn, helps to alleviate pain.

Soothing Tremors

Several studies conducted in Israel showed that the consumption of cannabis helps to reduce pain as well as the tremors associated with Parkinson's disease. In fact, it was also observed that cannabis improves the quality of sleep in those suffering from Parkinson's. Another notable discovery of this study was that the consumption of cannabis also helped in improving the motor skills among the patients who were a part of the study. Israel has legalized medical marijuana and a lot of continuous research is being conducted about the benefits of cannabis with the backing of the Israeli government

Crohn's Disease

Crohn's disease is a condition wherein an individual suffers from severe inflammatory bowel disorder accompanied by severe pain, diarrhea, nausea, vomiting, weight loss, and other troublesome symptoms. In a study that was conducted, it was discovered that the ingestion of cannabis via smoking helps to reduce the symptoms of Crohn's disease in the participants of the study. This was a rather small study, but a lot of researchers seem to agree that cannabis is an effective pain killer or suppressor and it can be quite helpful to those who suffer from painful conditions like Crohn's disease, multiple sclerosis, and so on. The cannabinoids from marijuana help to regulate the bacteria present in the gut and improve the function of the intestines. All this, in turn, helps to alleviate the painful symptoms associated with Crohn's disease.

Dravet's Syndrome

Dravet's Syndrome is a condition wherein a person suffers from seizures as well as developmental delays. Research was conducted on children suffering from Dravet's Syndrome who were offered medical marijuana with a high CBD and low THC content. According to this research, medical marijuana helped in reducing the seizures experienced by the participants.

Quitting Smoking and Drug Withdrawal

There is some evidence that is rather promising which shows that CBD present in cannabis can come in handy when people are trying to quit smoking. A pilot study showed that smokers who used an inhaler that had CBD present in it smoked fewer cigarettes than the ones who did not. Not just that, but CBD was also shown to help reduce nicotine addiction. Another similar study showed that CBD is quite helpful in reducing the symptoms of drug withdrawal. Researchers are of the opinion that some of the symptoms experienced by substance abuse users can be significantly reduced with the help of CBD. The symptoms that CBD helps rectify are anxiety, mood swings, pain, and insomnia. So, CBD can be used in reducing or even eliminating the symptoms of withdrawal.

Anxiety Disorders

Patients with chronic anxiety are often advised against consuming cannabis since the THC present in it can trigger or even amplify the paranoia that they might experience. However, a review presented in *Neurotherapeutics* suggests that while THC might amplify anxiety, CBD can help to reduce anxiety experienced by individuals suffering from any anxiety disorders. The research showed that CBD can help to reduce anxiety by calming the mind.

Reduces the Side Effects of Hepatitis C

The treatments available for Hepatitis C tend to produce rather severe side effects. In fact, the side effects can be so severe that at times patients aren't able to go through with their treatment. The common side effects include loss of appetite nausea, extreme fatigue, muscle pain, and even depression. However, by including cannabis as part of the treatment, the severity of these symptoms can be alleviated. In 2006, a study was published in the *European Journal of Gastroenterology and Hepatology* in which it was observed that over 80 percent of patients using cannabis were able to complete their treatment for Hepatitis C when compared to the existing rate of around 25 percent non-users of cannabis completing the necessary treatment. Cannabis also helps to improve the efficiency of Hepatitis C treatment.

Reducing the Side Effects of Chemotherapy

One of the most popular uses of medicinal marijuana is in combating the side effects of chemotherapy. Chemotherapy is the only means of slowing down or eliminating the growth of cancerous cells in the body. However, chemotherapy can take a toll on the health of the individual undergoing this therapy. The side effects of chemotherapy include extreme pain, severe nausea, and vomiting along with a loss of appetite. All these side effects can cause other health complications. Cannabis helps to reduce these side effects. As mentioned earlier, it is an effective means of reducing pain and nausea. Also, one of the effects of consuming cannabis is that it causes an increase in appetite, and this certainly comes in handy while treating chemotherapy patients

Acne

A study that was published by the *Journal of Clinical Investigation* and the National Institute of Health found that cannabis could be used to treat acne. Researchers used cannabis on the sebaceous glands and concluded that the chemical compound acts as an anti-inflammatory.

Diabetes

Diabetes develops in both people and animals. In a study conducted, cannabis was used on non-obese diabetic mice to see if it helped prevent the development of diabetes. There was no direct effect of cannabis on glucose levels; however, the treatment prevented the production of IL-12. It is essential to prevent this cytokine from being produced since it plays a huge role in the development of many autoimmune diseases.

Fibromyalgia

Opioid pain medications, corticosteroids, and anti-inflammatory medications are the most common methods used for treating fibromyalgia. A study conducted in 2011 focused on the effect of cannabis on patients who have fibromyalgia. The study showed promising results, which made way for the use of cannabis in future treatments. Fifty percent of the patients were subjected to cannabis treatment while the remaining 50 percent were subjected to traditional treatment. Those using cannabis showed significant improvement when compared to patients using traditional medication.

Cannabis can help treat a host of health problems. However, not many are comfortable with the idea of smoking cannabis. You no longer have to smoke cannabis to enjoy the benefits it offers! By using the simple recipes discussed in this book, you can reap all the benefits it offers without having to smoke it.

CHAPTER FIVE

SIDE EFFECTS OF CANNABIS

Now that you are aware of the various health benefits cannabis offers, in this section, you will learn about the different side effects the consumption of cannabis edibles can have on the body.

The effects that a cannabis user will experience depend on different factors like the dosage, the method with which cannabis is administered, any prior experience, level of tolerance, other drug use, personal expectations, state of mind, and the immediate environment as well as the individual's mood.

The short-term side effects of cannabis might or might not be experienced by all users. The consumption of cannabis can alter an individual's state of consciousness, as the user might experience a euphoric high and feel relaxed. It can also lead to the distortion of one's perception of space and time. The user might experience a sudden sensitivity to things around them and might even be able to experience things in a different manner. It can slightly alter an individual's primary senses like sight, taste, hearing, and smell. Other side effects include a spike in heart rate, bloodshot eyes, dilation of pupils, and an increase in appetite. Consumption of cannabis can also impair one's ability to concentrate and can inhibit the coordination between the body and the mind. Other negative side effects include anxiety, paranoia, panic, and self-consciousness.

A heavy dose of cannabis can lead to sedation, disorientation, and even toxic psychosis. It can also lead to severe mood swings, panic attacks and hallucinations. Therefore, it is always important that you calculate the right dosage before consuming cannabis. Start with a small dosage and you can gradually increase it until you find something that works for you.

The physical effects of cannabis can be experienced within a couple of minutes of its consumption. However, it can take anywhere between 10 to 30 minutes for it to be fully active, and these effects can last a couple of hours. THC is soluble in water, so it can also be stored by the fat cells within the body for a couple of months.

Apart from the short-term effects, consumption of cannabis can also have long-term effects. If the method of administration of cannabis is via smoking, then it can cause irritation of the lungs and increase the risk of contracting chronic bronchitis. Chronic use of cannabis can also lead to drug dependency. It can lead to a decrease in levels of concentration and the ability to remember things. Some people also experience a reduction in sex drive due to the constant and prolonged use of cannabis. Cannabis is a great way to deal with a lot of health conditions, but it is a good idea to consult your medical practitioner before you start using cannabis in any form.

There are a few things that you must absolutely avoid after administering cannabis. As mentioned earlier, it can lead to poor coordination. Therefore, please don't drive, operate any heavy machinery, or undertake the performance of hazardous activities after consuming cannabis. Cannabis can also lead to drowsiness and dizziness. Never consume any alcohol while using cannabis since this combination can lead to a severe loss of judgment and increase drowsiness or dizziness. Women must not use cannabis if they are pregnant, trying to become pregnant, or might become pregnant. The use of cannabis at the time of conception can increase the risk of birth defects. Also, women who are breastfeeding must not consume cannabis.

CHAPTER SIX

CALCULATING THC DOSAGE

If you want to cook edibles, then you need to learn to calculate the THC dosage. In fact, this is one topic that no home cook can afford to skip. If the THC dosage in the edibles is too high or low, you will not experience any of the benefits that are associated with cannabis edibles. For calculating the dosage, you must consider a couple of factors like the strength of the cannabis and your tolerance toward it. The ideal dosage is usually around 10 to 15 milligrams. However, when it comes to edibles, it is always a good idea to be aware of the THC content per serving. There is a simple formula that you can use to determine the THC content, regardless of whether the plant matter you are using has been tested in a lab or not. That said, please keep in mind that this isn't a foolproof formula and it will only help you figure out the THC or the CBD content per serving of the cannabis edibles you cook. So, read on to learn about this formula and the way in which you can use it.

A lot of people aren't aware of the THC content in the plant material that they use. The usual average of THC in cannabis is around 10 percent. The simple formula that you must keep in mind is:

One gram of cannabis = 1000 milligrams and THC content is 10 percent of 1,000 milligrams. So, one gram of cannabis contains about 100 milligrams of THC. Now, by using this number, you must calculate the quantity of THC that's present in the cannabutter or cannabis-infused oil you plan to use. For instance, let us assume that the recipe calls for an ounce (around 28 grams) of cannabis for making a cup of cannabutter. An ounce of cannabis contains about 2800 milligrams of THC. The THC content or potency of the recipe will depend on the amount of cannabutter or oil the recipe calls for. If you are baking one batch of cookies (36 cookies), then you need to use about half a cup of cannabutter and this means that the total THC content of the batch of cookies is 1400 milligrams. Now that you know the total THC content, you can easily calculate the THC per cookie by dividing the total THC by the number of cookies baked. So, in this scenario, the THC content per cookie is 1400 milligrams/36 cookies = 38.8 milligrams per cookie.

Estimate the THC content in the plant material you are using and then divide it by 100 to obtain the THC content of the cannabis per milligram. Once you have this number, calculate the THC content in the infusion you are using and the amount of cannabis-infused oil or butter that the recipe calls for. Finally, divide this by the number of servings you can make with the recipe in order to obtain the appropriate dosage. If you feel that the dosage of THC as suggested by the recipe is too high, then you can reduce the amount of cannabis oil or butter you plan on using. Similarly, if the dosage isn't sufficient, then you merely need to increase the amount of cannabis oil or butter you are using.

The chart in this section provides the THC content that's necessary for experiencing a mild to strong psychotropic cannabis effect. The numbers given in the chart are based on hashish and cannabis grown indoors. A variety that's grown indoor typically has THC content between eight to 16 percent. Varieties grown outdoors have a THC content anywhere between four to eight percent. An individual will need about 20 to 30 milligrams of THC per kilogram of body weight for experiencing a mild psychotropic effect of cannabis. For instance, if an individual's weight is around 50 kg (110 pounds), then the quantity of THC that's necessary for a mild psychotropic effect is between 10 to 15 milligrams. If you weigh more, then you must adjust the THC dosage accordingly. If you are just getting started, then I suggest that you follow the numbers given in the following chart.

Body Weight	Mild Effect	Medium - Strong Effect
110 pounds	0.013 to 0.019 g	0.026 to 0.038g
130 pounds	0.015 to 0.022g	0.030 g to 0.044g
155 pounds	0.018 to 0.027g	0.036 to 0.054g
175 pounds	0.020 to 0.030 g	0.020 to 0.030 g

NOTE: If you are just getting started with cannabis, it is best if you start out with a small dosage. Everyone reacts differently to different dosages. Like with any new product, you will need to see how your body reacts to it. Depending on that reaction, you can determine whether you want to increase or decrease the dosage. The right dosage of cannabis will vary from one person to another. As a rule of thumb, a bigger person might need a higher dosage of cannabis than a smaller person. With cannabis, you have the freedom to increase the dosage by a few milligrams at a time for meeting your personal needs. If you have any preexisting medical conditions, then you must always consult a health-care professional before taking cannabis. A doctor or a medical professional can tell you take cannabis and the dosage you need to get the most out of it. So always consult your doctor first.

CHAPTER SEVEN

INTRODUCTION TO DECARBOXYLATION

About Decarboxylation

If you are interested in consuming cannabis edibles, then you can either purchase the prepackaged stuff or make the edibles at home. The cannabis edibles available on the market are quite expensive and tend to have varying contents of THC. If you decide to make cannabis edibles at home, you will have absolute control over the quality of ingredients you use.

Have you ever come across any scenes in a movie where someone ends up eating raw marijuana to prevent getting caught? Their eyes tend to go wide, and a lot of dramatic gasping follows suit. Here's a spoiler alert: no such thing happens when you consume raw cannabis. Why doesn't anything as dramatic as what's shown in movies happen when you eat raw cannabis? The answer to this is a process known as decarboxylation. This is essential if you want to enjoy the psychoactive effect of cannabis. Cannabinoids that are present within the trichomes present in raw cannabis flowers contain an additional carboxyl ring that's known as COOH. For instance, THCA (tetrahydrocannabinolic acid) is synthesized by the plant within the trichomes present in cannabis flowers. The cannabis that's distributed through dispensaries tends to contain labels about plant materials' cannabinoid content. THCA usually accounts for a major portion of the cannabinoid present in cannabis products that haven't been decarboxylated. THCA has different benefits, but it isn't a psychoactive ingredient, and only after decarboxylation will it be transformed into THC, the ingredient responsible for the psychoactive benefits of cannabis.

Time and heat are the primary catalysts needed for decarboxylation. Partial decarboxylation takes place when you dry and cure cannabis for a long time. This is the reason why some cannabis can test positive for trace amounts of THC along with THCA. Smoking and vaporizing are two means through which decarboxylation instantly takes place.

Decarboxylated cannabinoids in a vaporized form can be readily absorbed by the lungs, but when it comes to edibles, the cannabinoids present take longer for our bodies to absorb. Heating the cannabinoids steadily at a low temperature allows decarboxylation to take place and activates the THC present. Once the THC is activated, then you can easily infuse the cannabis with other ingredients to cook edibles.

Steps for Decarboxylating Cannabis at Home

Here are some simple steps that you can follow for decarboxylating cannabis at home.

- Preheat the oven for 20 minutes at 225°F. Doing this helps remove any moisture from the oven.

- Line an oven-safe dish with parchment paper.

- Crush the buds by breaking them into smaller pieces and by getting rid of any unnecessary plant materials like seeds. Place the crushed buds on the parchment paper. Ensure that the buds aren't crowded and are evenly arranged on the paper.

- Place the plant material in the oven and allow it to bake at 250°F for about 25 minutes. The color of the cannabis will change from green to a shade of light brown.

- Once it has reached a light brown color, bake it for another 20 minutes or so, until the cannabis is medium brown in color. Keep checking on the cannabis every 10 minutes to ensure that it isn't burning.

- Remove the cannabis from the parchment paper and allow it to cool for a while. The cannabis will be quite crumbly and if you aren't careful while handling it, you will be left with powdered cannabis.

- Once it has cooled down, you can roughly grind it using a mortar and pestle. I prefer using a mortar and pestle or a manual weed crusher instead of a food processor. You need coarse flakes of cannabis, almost like oregano seasoning.

- Store the decarboxylated cannabis in an airtight container and keep it in a dry and dark place.

Please note that the decarboxylation process gives off a rather pungent herbal odor, so ensure that you turn on the exhaust fan in the kitchen!

CHAPTER EIGHT

COOKING WITH CANNABIS

In this section, you will learn about cooking with cannabis.

Cannabis Can Taste Good

If you aren't a fan of the woody and earthy aroma of cannabis, then you don't have to worry about it while cooking with cannabis. When you cook edibles, the original taste of cannabis will be overpowered by that of any other ingredient you use, such as chocolate or any other flavoring. Infusing cannabis with coconut oil, butter, or any other oil of your choice will give the oil or fat a rather nutty profile that perfectly complements any earthy spices like cinnamon, nutmeg, garlic, or any other spices that you can think of. Since the flavor of the bud is fully masked by any other flavorful ingredient you use, the edibles will not have any traces of the smell or flavor of weed. Once you infuse any oil or butter with cannabis, then you can start using that cannabis-infused butter for cooking savory dishes as well as desserts.

Not Limited to Heavy Foods

When you think of cannabis edibles, what is the first thing that pops into your head? Perhaps a cannabis-infused brownie? Who doesn't like a brownie? Just because you want to cook with cannabis, you don't have to use a lot of sugar or unnecessary calories. Most edibles that are readily available these days are full of processed sugars and carbs.

However, please understand that edibles don't have to be calorie-dense foods. Cannabis is quite a versatile ingredient and can be easily incorporated into any recipe. The slightly citrusy and herbal notes in marijuana are quite similar to the ones present in spices like pepper, mint, or rosemary. Therefore, it can be used in a similar fashion. All these flavors work well together, and they don't necessarily have to be used to cook calorie-rich foods. You can use cannabis-infused butter or oil to cook pretty much anything you want. You can use cannabis-infused olive oil as a dressing for salads!

Select the Right Strain

The strain of marijuana that you use will determine the effect the edibles will have on you. For instance, a cannabis strain like Hindu Kush will have a rather drowsy effect and you will experience the same effect if you cook using that strain. Any of the uplifting strains of sativa also tend to have the same effect. You must not forget all these things before you start cooking with it. For instance, if you want a boost of energy in the morning, then you can add a drop or two of cannabis-infused coconut oil to your cup of coffee. If you opt for an OG strain, you will make yourself quite drowsy. So, you need to opt for a strain that has an uplifting effect!

You can Combine it with Alcohol

THC can be infused with alcohol and not just fats. Infusing cannabis with liquor is quite similar to infusing any liquor with herbs. Take some crushed marijuana, add it to a bottle of whiskey, seal it tightly, and leave it undisturbed in a dark place for a couple of weeks! Once the weed is infused with the liquor, you can use the infused liquor to make delicious cocktails! However, you must keep in mind that the potency of liquor increases when you infuse it with marijuana.

You can infuse cannabis with either fat or an oil-based ingredient if you want to cook with it. The list of fats that you can use include butter, lard, ghee, shortening, and any other nut or vegetable oil. If the recipe you decide to use does not contain any fatty ingredients, then you can use any spirit (cognac, vodka, rum, and so on) to dilute the cannabis concentrate. Any water-based alcohol like wine or beer is not a good carrier for cannabis oil. You can use cannabis oil in sweet and savory recipes alike. Make sure that you measure the sweetening or the spice flavors in the recipe to reduce the natural bitterness of cannabis oil.

Include it in Your Meal

Try to think of the different ways in which you can incorporate cooking with marijuana into your regular meals. You can even incorporate it into different social activities like dinner parties. For instance, food that's infused with cannabis can be a wonderful culinary experience. It not only increases one's appetite, but it also allows people to thoroughly enjoy their food and creates a rather intense experience. You can serve a simple appetizer infused with some cannabis and it will enable your guests to enjoy the entrée with some extra relish.

Prepare it Beforehand

A common mistake that a lot of newbies cooking edibles make is that they mix cannabis with butter and add it to a saucepan before they cook. Well, this is a terrible idea for two reasons. The first reason is that doing this prevents you from capturing a significant portion of the active agent present in cannabis and the second reason is that you can easily burn the useful substances present in cannabis. If you want to make edibles, then you need to plan ahead and make butter or oil infused with cannabis well before you start cooking. Infusing cannabis with oil or butter is a slow process that must not be rushed. To protect THC or the active ingredient present in cannabis, you must let it simmer on extremely low heat for a long time or even use a water bath. Exposing THC to direct heat will burn it, and the infused oil or butter will not be potent.

Try Doing it Yourself

If you have never tried cannabis edibles before or are planning on eating edibles that you purchased, then please don't consume them on an empty stomach. Readymade cannabis edibles tend to be rather unpredictable and consuming them on an empty stomach can overwhelm your system. Therefore, if you are interested in consuming edibles, then the best thing that you can do is to start cooking them at home! By making edibles at home, you will have absolute control over the quality and quantity of ingredients that you use.

Tips for Troubleshooting

Now that you are aware of different things that you must keep in mind while buying cannabis, there are some mistakes that you must avoid while cooking with cannabis. In this section, you will learn about different tips that will come in handy while cooking with cannabis.

Don't grind it too much

Most of the recipes that you find online for edibles recommend finely grinding cannabis for making cannabis-infused oils or butter. In fact, some of the commercially manufactured electronic appliances used for making cannabutter come with an inbuilt grinder. This doesn't make any sense to me. If you want to cook edibles without compromising their taste or potency, then I suggest that you don't grind the plant material into a fine powder. The resin-like trichomes you are trying to extract are present on the buds and the leaves of the cannabis plant and not within. So, if you grind cannabis into a fine powder, then you will end up adding a lot more of the plant material into the edibles instead of just the useful trichomes. All this will give the edibles a rather pungent and herby flavor, along with a green hue to the finished product. If you don't want the edibles to be unappetizing, then please don't grind the plant material into a fine powder.

Add water while infusing cannabis

A common mistake that a lot of people make is that they don't add any water while making cannabutter or cannabis-infused oil. I think it is a good idea to add some water to the cannabis and butter or oil mixture, especially if you want to cook it on the stovetop. Water enables you to infuse cannabis at a low temperature and it also prevents the cannabis from burning. If the plant material burns or gets scorched, then the active ingredient—the THC present in it—will be lost and it lends a rather unappetizing flavor to the edibles. If the active ingredient is lost, then the cannabis-infused oil or butter will not have any potency. Also, by adding water, you can eliminate some of the green color and herby flavor of cannabis. There is no hard and fast rule about the amount of water that you need to add, but I personally suggest adding water and butter or oil in equal proportions (a 1:1 ratio is ideal).

Cooking at a high temperature

As a rule of thumb, it is always advisable to cook cannabis at low temperatures. The THC tends to completely disintegrate if the cooking temperature exceeds 390°F. In fact, THC starts to disintegrate well before that. The temperature at which water starts to boil is around 212°F, so it is a good idea to add water while cooking with cannabis. Also, if you are cooking with infused oils or butter or any other marijuana concentrates, you need to keep an eye on the temperature. Never directly use cannabis-infused oils or butter while sautéing or frying anything. You must not expose cannabis-infused oils or butter to direct heat. You can add them to the batter and then cook the batter. Ensure that the oven temperature doesn't exceed 375°F. At this temperature, the food cooks, but THC doesn't disintegrate.

Always decarb cannabis

Excess heat will destroy THC in cannabis, but you need some heat to activate it. A lot of people fail to realize that raw marijuana plant material barely contains any THC. It contains THC acid and then you need to convert this THC acid into THC by a process known as decarboxylation. Take a moment to think about it; even if you want to smoke cannabis, you need to light the joint! The heat helps activate THC and without the heat, this chemical will stay inactive. When you infuse butter or oil with cannabis, then a portion of the decarb process is taken care of while infusing cannabis into the fat you desire. However, if you want to increase the potency of THC in the plant material, then you need to decarb it first. Not just kief, but even hash must be decarboxylated before you cook with it to increase its potency!

Adding too much marijuana

The easiest way to ingest cannabis is by eating it. At times people tend to get impatient, start thinking that the edibles aren't working, and overeat. Well, by the time the THC kicks in, they realize that they probably ate more than desired. Overdosing on cannabis is hardly ever fatal, but it can certainly increase paranoia and disorientation. Getting the dosage right is quite important when it comes to edibles. In fact, I think it is a bit of an art since there are a lot of different things that you must consider while deciding the dosage. The effect that cannabis has differs from one person to another. For instance, a dosage that might not even have a physical effect on one person might make someone else extremely drowsy. Different things like a person's capacity and tolerance towards marijuana determine the effect the plant material has on their body. If you aren't familiar with cooking with any plant material, then I suggest that you try vaping or smoking beforehand to determine its potency. Please remember that cooking cannabis increase its potency. If the batch you cook is quite potent, then you simply need to regulate the portions you consume.

Adding too little

Adding too much or too little cannabis will not give you the desired effect. If the cannabis oil or butter that you make is not as potent as you hoped, then you can always tweak it. You simply need to slowly reheat the cannabis oil or butter and add some more decarboxylated kief or hash to that mixture. You might be tempted to add as little cannabis as possible since it is an expensive ingredient, but don't let this urge control you. If the oil or butter is too potent, then you merely need to use smaller quantities of it! However, cooking with cannabis-infused oil or butter that isn't potent will certainly yield disappointing results.

Cleanliness matters

This might sound like a rather obvious thing, but please ensure that the cooking station is clean to prevent any contamination. You don't want to find any bread crumbs or cat hair in the cannabis edibles you cook, do you? The cooking equipment and the cooking station must be clean. To prevent cross-contamination, I suggest that you use a different set of kitchen equipment for cooking cannabis.

Sweet and savory recipes

You can infuse cannabis either with fat or with an oil-based ingredient if you want to cook with it. The list of fats you can use includes butter, lard, ghee, shortening, and other nuts or vegetable oil. If your chosen recipe does not contain fat, you can dilute the hemp concentrate with any alcohol (brandy, vodka, rum, etc.). Aqueous alcohol, such as wine or beer, is not a good carrier for hemp oil. You can use cannabis oil in both sweet and spicy recipes. Be sure to measure the sweetness or spice of flavors in a recipe to reduce the natural bitterness of hemp oil.

Control heat

Cannabis extraction is reduced when exposed to direct heat. If you don't put cannabis-rich fat right on a hot frying pan or frying pan, that's fine. The fat or oil you use should be at the same temperature as tea or coffee (160 to 185). If you use hemp drenched in alcohol, you do not need to preheat the alcohol.

Choose wisely

Carefully select the concentrate and measure the active ingredient before you start cooking. Always start small. Then you can gradually increase the level of concentrate in the recipe. Until you understand your ideal dosage, it is advisable to use a small amount of cannabis extract.

Marijuana is commonly referred to as an illegal drug. But edible marijuana is usually a prescribed medicine. The edible leaf is used to cure and suppress a variety of diseases. The preferred means of taking marijuana is through smoking, but only a few people know that you can cook with cannabis. The cooking procedure might seem intimidating and requires a lot of patience. It's not as simple as grinding the leaves and adding the hash but has a few rules that you must follow. You will learn more about all this in the coming chapters in the book.

CHAPTER NINE

CANNABIS-INFUSED BASIC RECIPES

How to Decarb Cannabis:

Place a sheet of parchment paper on a baking sheet. Spread cannabis all over the sheet.

Place it in a preheated oven at 220°F for 35-60 minutes. Remove from the oven. This is what you call decarboxylated or decarbed marijuana/cannabis. Use this procedure when decarbed cannabis is mentioned in any of the recipes in this book.

Always adjust the cannabis according to your personal needs*

Cannabis Tincture

Cooking time: NA

Ingredients:

- 2 ounces cannabis, finely ground, decarbed

- 2 quarts grain alcohol like Everclear

Method:

1   Sanitize a 2-quart glass jar or mason jar.

2   Add marijuana to the jar.

3   Fill the jar with alcohol.

4   Fasten the lid and place in a cool, dark place. Shake the jar every couple of days. Repeat this process for 2-3 weeks.

5   Strain with a cheesecloth or a fine wire mesh strainer into a jar. Pour into dropper bottles. Place in the refrigerator or a cool place until use.

6   Use as directed by your doctor.

Cannabutter / Margarine

Cooking time: 45-50 minutes

Ingredients:

- 1/2 ounce cannabis buds, finely ground

- 1 cup butter/margarine/vegan butter

Method:

1   Place a saucepan over low heat. Add butter or margarine. When the butter or margarine melts, add cannabis powder and stir frequently with a wooden spoon.

2   Let simmer for about 45-50 minutes. Turn off the heat.

3   Strain into a glass container that has a fitted lid. Press the residue with the back of a spoon. Discard the residue.

4   When the butter hardens, place in the refrigerator until use. If you want to make a larger quantity of butter, cook for 60-70 minutes. After the butter hardens, pour some water into the container to cover the butter. This way it lasts longer.

Cannabis-Infused Cooking Oil

Cooking time: 3 hours

Ingredients:

- 32 ounces cooking oil like olive oil or avocado oil or canola oil

- 1/2 ounce cannabis, decarbed

Method:

1   Place a saucepan over low heat. Add oil and warm.

2   Stir in the cannabis.

3   Cook for about 3 hours, stirring every 30 minutes. Don't let the oil simmer or boil.

4   Place cheesecloth over a fine wire mesh strainer, placed on a large heatproof bowl.

5   Strain the oil in a bowl using cheesecloth. Squeeze the cheesecloth to remove as much oil as possible.

6   Let the oil come to room temperature. Pour into an airtight container and use as required.

Canna-Flour

Cooking time: NA

Ingredients

- 2 cups all-purpose flour

- 1/2 ounce cannabis, decarbed, finely ground

Method:

1 Add flour and cannabis to a mixing bowl. Whisk until well incorporated either with a spatula or electric hand mixer with a whisk attachment.

2 Transfer to an airtight container. Place in a cool and dry place until use. It can last for 3 months.

Cannabis Milk

Cooking time: 1 hour

Ingredients

- Water, as required

- 5 cups milk (use 2 1/2 cups per serving)

- 1/2 ounce marijuana leaves (use 1/4 ounce per serving)

Method:

1   Place a pot of water over low heat. Add marijuana leaves and simmer for 10-12 minutes.

2   Turn off the heat and drain the water. Keep the marijuana leaves in the pot.

3   Add milk and simmer on low heat for about 35-40 minutes. Stir frequently.

4   Simmer until the milk is reduced to nearly half its original quantity.

5   Strain through a fine wire mesh strainer placed over a bowl.

6   Serve hot or chill and serve later.

Marijuana Honey

Cooking time: 4 hours

Ingredients

- pounds honey

- 1/2 ounce marijuana (half of the sugar shack and half the bud) discard stems, crushed

Method

1. Take a large piece of cheesecloth and fold in the center to make a double layer. Place the marijuana in it. Roll the cheesecloth. Seal the marijuana well. It shouldn't come out of the cloth. Fasten with string at the center and the sides.

2. Pour honey in a crockpot. Place the cheesecloth bag in it.

3. Cover and cook on lowest setting for 4 hours. Stir every hour. The color of the honey will have darkened by the end of 4 hours. Make sure that the honey does not boil. Keep it on a very low setting.

4. Let the honey remain in the crockpot overnight.

5. Heat the honey slightly if the honey is not pourable. Remove the cheesecloth bag and squeeze with your hands. Let the drippings drop into the honey. Stir well.

6. Pour into airtight containers. Store in a cool and dry place.

Weed Sugar

Cooking time: 1 hour

Ingredients:

- 0.2 ounce cannabis, decarbed

- 7 ounces granulated sugar

- 1 cup high-proof, unflavored alcohol like Everclear

Method:

1. Add cannabis to a glass jar. Pour alcohol in it. Fasten the lid and shake the jar well every 5 minutes, for 20 minutes.

2. Strain the alcohol by passing through cheesecloth. Squeeze the cheesecloth to remove as much alcohol as possible. Discard the cannabis.

3. Preheat oven to 200°F.

4. Mix together sugar and strained alcohol in a baking dish. Stir until sugar dissolves completely.

5. Bake at 200°F.

6. Stir the mixture every 10-12 minutes for an hour or until dry and the sugar crystalizes again.

7. Remove from the oven and cool completely.

8. Store in an airtight container.

Coconut Cannabis Oil

Cooking time: 4-24 hours

Ingredients:

- 10 cups distilled water

- 2 cups organic coconut oil

- 4 ounces cannabis, finely ground

Method:

1. Add coconut oil into a crockpot.

2. Set the crockpot on the lowest setting and melt the oil.

3. Stir in water and cannabis and mix until well incorporated.

4. Set the crockpot on high setting. Let the mixture heat for 1 hour. Stir often.

5. Change the crockpot setting to low. Let the mixture infuse for 4-24 hours. Stir after every 50-60 minutes.

6. Place cheesecloth over a fine wire mesh strainer, placed over a large heatproof bowl.

7. Strain the oil in the bowl using a cheesecloth. Squeeze the cheesecloth to remove as much oil as possible.

8. Let the oil come to room temperature. Pour into an airtight container and refrigerate for 8-9 hours.

9. The oil will have hardened by now. Drain off the water and use the oil as required.

Cannabis Mayonnaise

Cooking time: NA

Ingredients

- 2 eggs

- 2 teaspoons prepared yellow mustard

- 2 tablespoons lemon juice

- 1 1/2 cups cannabis-infused oil

- 1 teaspoon minced garlic

- Salt and pepper to taste

Method

1. Blend together eggs, lemon juice, mustard, garlic, salt, and pepper in a blender. Blend until smooth.

2. While the blender is running on low speed, pour the cannabis-infused oil in a thin stream until the mayonnaise is emulsified and thick.

3. Transfer to an airtight container and refrigerate until use.

Cannabis Peanut Butter

Cooking time: NA

Ingredients

- 3 teaspoons cannabis-infused extra-virgin olive oil

- 4 tablespoons peanut butter

Method

1. Add oil peanut butter to a jar or bowl.

2. Mix well with a spoon until smooth and creamy.

Canna-Cream Cheese

Cooking time: 30-40 minutes

Ingredients:

- 1/2 gallon whole milk

- 1/4 teaspoon salt

- 1/2 quart cultured buttermilk

- 1/2 ounce cannabis, finely ground

Method:

1. Add milk and buttermilk to a saucepan. Heat the saucepan on a medium flame. Stir occasionally until the temperature of the milk shows 170°F on a candy thermometer.

2. Let the mixture simmer between 170°F and 175°F for around 12-15 minutes. Turn the heat off when the milk mixture begins to separate into curds.

3. Place many layers of cheesecloth inside a strainer. Place the strainer on a bowl.

4. Pass the mixture through the strainer. Retain the curds and use the milk that is remaining in some other recipe or discard it.

5. Cool the curds completely in the strainer.

6. Transfer to a blender. Add salt and blend until smooth.

7. Transfer to an airtight container and chill until use. It can last for 3-4 days.

Marijuana Vinaigrette

Cooking time: NA

Ingredients:

- 1/2 teaspoon minced garlic

- 1 teaspoon fresh basil or oregano or ½ teaspoon basil or oregano

- 7-8 tablespoons cannabis-infused oil

- 1/2 tablespoon red onion or shallot, minced

- 2 tablespoons balsamic vinegar or any other vinegar of your choice

- Salt to taste

- Pepper to taste

Method:

1. Add salt, pepper, garlic, oregano or basil, onion, and vinegar into a blender and blend until it become smooth.

2. While the blender is running, pour cannabis-infused oil in a thin stream. Blend until the vinaigrette is slightly thick. If your vinaigrette is not thickening, add more oil until the desired thickness is achieved.

3. Transfer to a bowl or jar. Add salt and pepper to taste.

4. Use in salads.

CHAPTER TEN

MUNCHIES

Sweet Potato Fries

Serves: 2-3

Cooking time: 20-30 minutes

Ingredients:

- 1 pound sweet potatoes (the orange variety), peeled if desired

- Sea salt to taste

- 1 small clove garlic, finely minced

- 1 tablespoon cannabis-infused extra-virgin olive oil

- 1 tablespoon flat leaf parsley, chopped

- 2 tablespoons parmesan cheese, grated

Method:

1. Preheat oven to 450°F.

2. Rinse the sweet potato pieces and dry by patting with kitchen or paper towels.

3. Cut the sweet potatoes into fries.

4. Spread the sweet potatoes on a baking sheet.

5. Sprinkle salt and oil all over them. Toss well. Spread evenly all over the baking sheet, without overlapping.

6. Bake for 20 to 30 minutes.

7. Meanwhile, add garlic, parsley, and cheese into a bowl and stir.

8. When the fries are ready, transfer to the bowl of cheese and toss well.

9. Serve right away.

Weed Biscuits

Serves: 25-30

Cooking time: 12-15 minutes

Ingredients:

- 1 1/2 cups boiled, mashed sweet potatoes

- 2 tablespoons baking powder

- 3/4 cup cannabutter, unsalted, cold, cut into small cubes

- 1-2 cups milk

- 4 tablespoons sugar

- 2 teaspoons salt

- 3 cups all-purpose flour

Method:

1. Preheat oven to 425°F.

2. Add milk and sweet potatoes to a bowl and whisk well.

3. Mix together baking powder, sugar, salt, and flour in a bowl.

4. Add butter and mix using a fork or a pastry cutter until crumbly.

5. Mix the sweet potato batter and fold. If you find the mixture too very dry, then add some more milk.

6. Form into a smooth dough using your hands.

7. Roll the dough with a rolling pin. Chop into the desired shape with a cookie cutter. Re-roll the scrap dough and cut out some

more biscuits.

8. Gently lift the biscuits and place on a greased baking sheet, in a single layer. Bake in batches. Leave some gap between the biscuits.

9. Bake at 425°F for 12 to 15 minutes or until slightly hard and golden brown.

10. Remove from the oven and cool completely.

11. Transfer to an airtight container. Store at room temperature.

Baked Apricot Brie

Serves: 20-25

Cooking time: 30-40 minutes

Ingredients:

- 2 brie rounds (8 ounces each)

- 2 cups cannabutter, melted

- 1/4 teaspoon salt

- 1 package filo dough sheets, thawed

- 2/3 cup apricot preserves or orange marmalade

- 1/2 cup roasted, salted, chopped almonds (optional)

Method:

1. Preheat oven to 375°F.

2. Cut the outer rind off the brie. You can use it in some other recipe if desired or discard it. Set aside.

3. Add cannabutter into a saucepan. Place over low heat until it melts. Turn off the heat.

4. Unfold the filo dough.

5. Pull out 2 filo sheets and place on your countertop, slightly overlapping at the edges. You should have a rectangle of approximately 24 x 17 inches.

6. Brush melted butter over the filo sheets.

7. Place 2 more filo sheets over this, again slightly overlapping at the edges.

8. Repeat step 5-6. You should have at least 3 to 4 layers in all. The topmost layer should be brushed with butter.

9. Place one brie round in the center of the filo rectangle.

10. Smear 5-6 tablespoons of the apricot preserves over the brie.

11. Sprinkle salt and half the almonds.

12. Fold the edges of the filo layers over the brie, to cover it completely. Press the edges to seal.

13. Repeat steps 2 to 11 and make the other brie.

14. Place on a lined baking sheet, with the seam side facing down.

15. Bake for 30 to 40 minutes or until golden brown. You may find that the brie is coming out of the pressed edges.

16. Remove from the oven and let cool for 15 minutes.

17. Cut into slices and serve with crackers of your choice.

Cannabis Granola

Serves: 40-50

Cooking time: 30 minutes

Ingredients:

1. 1 cup marijuana-infused coconut oil

2. 2 cups chopped mixed nuts

3. 2 teaspoons baking soda

4. 3 teaspoons ground cinnamon

5. Flavoring of your choice like vanilla extract, strawberry extract, etc. (optional)

6. 1 cup brown flaxseed meal

7. 1 cup honey or maple syrup

8. 1/8 teaspoon salt

9. 6 cups oatmeal

10. 1 cup berries or fruits of your choice

Method:

1. Preheat oven to 300°F.

2. Line 2 large rimmed baking sheets with parchment paper. Add oatmeal, flaxseed meal, nuts, and cinnamon into a bowl and mix well.

3. If the oil is solid, then melt it either in a microwave or on the stovetop in a saucepan.

4. Whisk together oil, salt, honey, and any flavoring if using. Pour

into the bowl of oatmeal mixture.

5. Mix until well incorporated. Transfer onto baking sheets. Spread evenly. Bake in batches.

6. Bake at 300°F for 20-30 minutes or until golden brown. Stir once, halfway through baking.

7. Remove the baking sheet from the oven and mix in the berries. Spread again on the baking sheet evenly.

8. Let cool slightly. Cut into bars. You can also make balls of the granola or any other shape of your choice.

9. Transfer to an airtight container and refrigerate until use.

Super Lemon Haze Mexican Guacamole

Serves: 8

Cooking Time: NA

Ingredients:

- 8 Hass avocados, peeled, pitted, mashed

- 4 small heads garlic, peeled, minced

- 2 cups small cherry tomatoes, finely chopped

- 2 sweet white onions, chopped

- Juice of 2 limes

- 2 ounces cannabis olive oil

- 2 teaspoons chili powder or to taste

- Cracked pepper to taste

- 2 teaspoons paprika or to taste

- 1 teaspoon cayenne pepper or to taste

- Sea salt to taste

Method:

1. Mix all the ingredients in a bowl and stir well until thoroughly combined.

2. Cover and chill for a while in order to allow the flavors to mingle.

3. Serve with vegetable sticks or crackers.

Stuffed Mini Peppers

Serves: 8 (4 pepper halves per serving)

Cooking time: 20 minutes

Ingredients:

- 16 mini peppers, split, deseeded

- 2 chorizo sausages, thinly sliced

- 2 teaspoons garlic, minced

- Salt to taste

- Pepper to taste

- 6-8 tablespoons cannabis-infused olive oil

- 10 scallions, sliced

- 3 cups fresh bread crumbs

- 4-6 tablespoons crumbled goat cheese

- 1-2 tablespoons olive oil, if required

Method:

1. Preheat oven to 300°F.

2. Line a large baking sheet with parchment paper.

3. Place pepper halves on it.

4. Place a pan over medium heat. Add oil and heat. When the oil is heated, add chorizo and cook for a few minutes. Remove the chorizo along with the cooked oil into a bowl. Set aside.

5. Place the pan back over medium heat.

6. Stir in the scallions into the pan. Cook for 2 to 3 minutes. Stir in garlic, salt, pepper, and bread crumbs. Mix well. Stir in some olive oil if the mixture is looking very dry.

7. Add chorizo along with the oil and mix well. Fill the pepper halves with this mixture. Press the filling well into the peppers.

8. Place some goat cheese on top of each pepper.

9. Bake for 20-30 minutes until the cheese is golden brown.

Monster Munchie Balls

Serves: 20-25

Cooking time: 8-10 minutes

Ingredients:

- 3/4 cup cannabutter

- 2 tablespoons chunky peanut butter

- 1 tablespoon cocoa powder or chocolate syrup

- 1 1/2 cups rolled oats or granola

- 1 1/2 tablespoons honey

Method:

1. Add cannabutter to a saucepan. Place saucepan over low heat. Add the remaining ingredients and stir constantly until well incorporated. Cook for a couple of minutes. Stir constantly.

2. Transfer to a baking dish. Cool slightly. Freeze for 10-12 minutes until semi-soft in consistency.

3. Scoop with an ice-cream scoop and place in an airtight container lined with wax paper.

Note: First-timers should not eat more than half a scoop.

Hialeah Hash Browns

Serves: 4-5

Cooking time: 15 minutes

Ingredients:

- 1 pound fresh malangas, peeled, chopped, or grated

- Hash-butter to fry

- 2 eggs

- Salt and pepper to taste

- 1/2 teaspoon garlic powder

Method:

1. Add eggs, malangas, salt, garlic, and pepper into a bowl and mix until well combined.

2. Chill for an hour.

3. Place a deep pan over medium flame. Add hash-butter and let heat. Make small balls of the mixture.

4. When the butter melts, add a few of the malanga balls and fry until they turn golden brown and crisp.

5. Remove and place on a plate.

6. Fry the rest in batches.

7. Serve with a dip of your choice.

CHAPTER ELEVEN

BREAKFAST RECIPES

Banana Nut Bread

Serves: 20-25

Cooking time: 60-90 minutes

Ingredients:

- 1 cup brown sugar

- 1 cup granulated sugar

- 2 eggs

- 2 teaspoons milk

- 2 teaspoons ground cinnamon

- 2 teaspoons baking powder

- 2 teaspoons baking soda

- 1 cup chocolate chips

- 1 cup cannabutter

- 6 bananas, peeled, mashed

- 1 cup walnuts, chopped

- 1 teaspoon vanilla extract

- 3 cups flour

- 1 cup whole-wheat flour

- 2 teaspoons baking powder

Method:

1. Preheat oven to 325°F.

2. Add cannabutter, brown sugar, and sugar to a mixing bowl and beat with an electric hand mixer until creamy.

3. Add eggs at a time and beat well each time.

4. Beat until the mixture is light and creamy. Set aside for a while.

5. Mix together whole-wheat flour, baking soda, baking powder, flour, and cinnamon in a bowl and set aside.

6. Add bananas, vanilla, and milk into a bowl and beat until well combined. Pour into the bowl of butter mixture.

7. Whisk until well combined.

8. Add the mixture of dry ingredients mixture into it and mix well.

9. Add the walnuts and chocolate chips and mix well.

10. Pour into a greased baking pan or large loaf pan.

11. Bake at 325°F for 1 to 1 1/2 hours or until brown on top.

12. Cool on your countertop for 15 minutes.

13. Invert onto a plate. Cool until warm.

14. Slice and serve.

Weed French Toast

Serves: 8 (2 toasts each)

Cooking time: 45 minutes

Ingredients:

- 8 eggs

- 16 slices, sliced crosswise, from French baguette

- 6 tablespoons cannabutter

- 3 tablespoons butter, unsalted, plus extra for greasing

- 1 1/2 cups milk

- 1 1/2 teaspoons vanilla extract

- 5 tablespoons maple syrup

- 1 1/2 cups milk

- 1/3 cup sugar

- 3/4 teaspoon salt

- Powdered sugar

Method:

1. Preheat oven to 350°F.

2. Grease the baking dish with butter.

3. Add both the butters to a bowl and mix well. Spread this mixture on one side of each slice of bread.

4. Lay the bread slices in the baking dish, buttered side facing up.

5. Whisk together the rest of the ingredients in a bowl until well combined.

6. Pour this mixture over the bread slices. Press down with a spoon.

7. Cover and chill overnight.

8. Bake for about 45 minutes or until it turns golden brown.

9. Remove from oven and cool for 5 minutes.

10. Sprinkle powdered sugar and serve.

Krispy Kreme Doughnuts

Serves: 20-25

Cooking time: 20-30 minutes

Ingredients:

For donuts:

- 6 tablespoons milk

- 2 teaspoons dry active yeast

- 6 tablespoons sugar

- 4 tablespoons butter, at room temperature

- Oil to fry, as required

- 6 tablespoons boiling water

- 3 cups all-purpose flour or more if required

- 2 eggs, slightly beaten

- 1/4 teaspoon salt

For glaze:

- 2/3 cup cannabutter

- 3 teaspoons vanilla extract

- 4 cups confectioners' sugar

- 8 tablespoons water, or as required

Method:

1. Add boiling water and milk into a large bowl. Stir in 1/2

tablespoon sugar and yeast. Set aside in a warm place for 10-15 minutes or until frothy.

2. Add flour, remaining sugar, and salt into a bowl and mix well. Add butter and cut into the mixture with pastry cutter or using your hands, until crumbly.

3. Stir in the eggs and yeast solution and stir until smooth dough is formed.

4. Dust your countertop with some flour. Place the dough on your countertop and knead the dough for 8-10 minutes until supple. Tiny bubbles should be visible on the underside.

5. Place the dough in the mixing bowl. Cover with cling wrap and let sit until it rises and is around twice its original size.

6. Divide the dough into 7-8 pieces. Pull each piece until it is about 1 to 1 1/2 inches width and a long log.

7. Cut into 1-inch pieces. Shape into donuts. Place on a baking sheet. Cover with some cloth and set aside. In a while, the donuts will rise.

8. Place a deep pan over medium heat. Pour enough oil to cover at least 3 inches of the pan. Let the oil heat.

9. When the temperature of the oil reaches 375°F, carefully lower a few donuts at a time into the oil. Fry until golden brown. Remove with a slotted spoon and place on a plate lined with paper towels.

10. Fry the remaining dough in batches.

11. Meanwhile, add all the ingredients for glaze into a saucepan and place over medium heat. Stir frequently until sugar dissolves completely. Turn off the heat. Cool for 5-8 minutes.

12. Dip the donuts in the glaze and place on a wire rack or on a

plate lined with paper towels.

13. If the glaze has turned cold, heat again until warm.

14. Serve warm or at room temperature.

Breakfast "Baked" Burritos

Serves: 2

Cooking time: 15 minutes

Ingredients:

- 2 eggs

- 2 flour tortillas (10 inches each)

- 1 1/2 ounces cheddar cheese, shredded

- 1 tablespoon cannabutter

- 3 ounces bacon, cut into strips

- 6-7 tablespoons refried beans

Method:

1. Place a large deep skillet over medium heat. Add the bacon and cook until crisp.

2. Remove on a plate lined with paper tissues so they soak the oil.

3. Wrap the tortillas in foil and heat in the oven.

4. Place a nonstick skillet over medium heat. Add cannabutter.

5. When the butter melts, crack and fry the eggs according to the way you like them cooked.

6. Place the warmed tortillas on your countertop.

7. Spread refried beans over the tortillas. Place a few strips of bacon and an egg on each tortilla.

8. Sprinkle cheese, roll, and serve.

Canna-Scrambler

Serves: 2

Cooking time: 15-17 minutes

Ingredients:

- 1 tablespoon cannabutter

- Salt to taste

- 4 eggs

- 1/2 cup milk

- Pepper to taste

Method:

1. Preheat oven to 350°F.

2. Add cannabutter to a baking dish.

3. Place the baking dish in oven for 5 minutes or until the butter melts.

4. Add salt, pepper, and eggs into a bowl. Whisk well. Add milk, a little at a time, and whisk well each time.

5. Transfer to the baking dish.

6. Bake in oven for 10 minutes.

7. Stir and bake until the eggs are cooked to the desired doneness.

8. Serve immediately.

Cannabis Breakfast Egg Cups

Serves: 6

Cooking time: 15-20 minutes

Ingredients:

- 6 sandwich bread slices

- 3/4 cup shredded cheddar cheese

- Pepper to taste

- Salt to taste

- 6 slices bacon, cooked, crumbled

- 2 tablespoons melted cannabutter

- 6 eggs

- 1 tablespoon minced fresh thyme

- Canna-oil, to grease

Method:

- Preheat oven to 375°F.

- Grease a six-count muffin pan with some canna-oil.

- Place bread slices on countertop. Roll with a rolling pin until flat.

- Cut each slice of bread into 2 equal triangles.

- Place 2 pieces of bread (triangles) in each cup on the bottom as well as the sides.

- Brush melted cannabutter over the slices.

- Bake at 375°F for 7-8 minutes.

- Divide the cheddar cheese among the muffin cups.

- Crack an egg into each cup. Sprinkle salt and pepper over it.

- Bake until the eggs are cooked to the desired doneness.

Canna-Cheesy Egg Benedict

Serves: 8

Cooking time: 20 minutes

Ingredients:

- 2 tablespoons cannabutter

- 1 1/2 cups milk

- 2 tablespoons shredded parmesan cheese,

- 4 tablespoons shredded cheddar cheese

- 3 1/2 tablespoons all-purpose flour

- 1/2 teaspoon Dijon mustard

- Salt to taste

- White pepper to taste

<u>For the poached eggs</u>

- 1 teaspoon white vinegar

- 4 English muffins, split, toasted

- 8 strips bacon, cooked, crumbled

- 8 cold eggs

- 8 slices Canadian bacon, warmed

Method:

1. To make cheese sauce: Place a saucepan over medium heat. Add cannabutter and melt. Add flour and stir for a few

seconds.

2. Pour the milk slowly, stirring simultaneously. Simmer until the sauce becomes thick. Stir constantly all the while.

3. Lower the heat. Add cheese, salt, pepper, and Dijon mustard and continue mixing until the cheese starts melting.

4. Remove from heat. Cover and set aside.

5. Place a large deep skillet over medium heat. Pour enough water in to cover about 3 inches from the bottom of the skillet.

6. Add vinegar and bring to the boil.

7. Crack an egg into a cup. Slowly slide the egg into the boiling water.

8. Repeat the previous step with the remaining eggs (add only as many eggs that can fit in the skillet) cook the rest in batches.

9. Cook until the eggs are set.

10. Place a Canadian bacon slice over each of the muffin halves. Place a poached egg over the bacon.

11. Spoon some cheese sauce over it.

12. Finally, place the crumbled bacon over it and serve.

Denver Omelet

Serves: 4

Cooking time: 12-15 minutes

Ingredients:

- 6 large eggs
- 1 cup chopped red or green bell pepper
- 8 slices bacon
- 1 teaspoon salt or to taste
- 1 cup chopped onion
- 1 cup cooked diced ham
- 2 tablespoons cannabutter
- 1 teaspoon pepper or to taste

Method:

1. Place a skillet over low heat. Add butter and melt. When butter melts, add onion, ham, pepper, and bacon and cook for a few minutes until vegetables are tender.

2. Meanwhile, whisk eggs and season with salt and pepper.

3. Spread the meat and vegetables in the skillet. Pour the eggs into the skillet. Cook them until the underside is golden brown. Flip and cook until the other side is golden brown.

4. Carefully slide the omelet onto a plate. Cut into 4 wedges and serve.

Oatmeal Pancakes

Serves: 6-8

Cooking time: 20-30 minutes

Ingredients:

- 2 tablespoons ghee (clarified butter)

- 2 cups rolled oats

- 2 tablespoons nut butter

- 8-16 drops cannabis tincture

- 2 ripe bananas, peeled, sliced

- 2 large eggs

- 2 tablespoons honey

Method:

1. Add banana, eggs, oats, and tincture into a blender and blend until smooth.

2. Pour the batter into a bowl.

3. Place a skillet over medium heat. Add about 1/4 tablespoon ghee and let it melt.

4. Pour about 1/4 cup batter on the pan. Bubbles will appear on the pancake. Cook until golden brown on the bottom. Flip sides and cook until the other side turns golden brown. Remove the pancake from the pan.

5. Repeat steps 3-4 and make the remaining pancakes.

6. Serve with honey or nut butter or any other toppings of your

choice.

Potffles (Medicated Waffles)

Serves: 5-6

Cooking time: 25-30 minutes

Ingredients:

- 1 egg

- 1 cup cannaflour

- 3 tablespoons melted cannabutter (or regular butter if desired)

- 1/2 teaspoon salt

- 2 teaspoons baking powder

- 1 teaspoon granulated sugar

- 3/4 cup warm milk

Method:

1. Add flour, salt, baking powder, and sugar to a bowl and stir until the mixture comes together.

2. Add egg in another bowl and whip lightly. Add milk and cannabutter and stir.

3. Pour this batter in the bowl of flour and beat well. The batter should not be very smooth. It should have a few lumps here and there.

4. Pour a ladle of batter into a preheated waffle iron. Cook until golden brown.

5. Repeat the previous step and make the remaining waffles.

Weed Bread

Serves: 25-30 slices

Cooking time: 40-50 minutes

Ingredients:

- 0.35 ounces marijuana flowers, deseeded, de-stemmed, ground coarsely

- Flaxseed meal or cornmeal for dusting

- 1/2 teaspoon active dry yeast

- 6 cups all-purpose flour or 4 cups flour and 2 cups whole-wheat flour

- 2 1/2 teaspoons salt

- 3 1/2 cups lukewarm water (110°F)

Method:

1. Add marijuana flowers, yeast, flour, and salt to a mixing bowl. Whisk until well combined. Add lukewarm water and mix to form sticky dough.

2. Cover the bowl with cling wrap and keep it in a warm place for 12-16 hours or until the dough doubles in size and tiny bubbles may be visible on the top of the dough.

3. Dust your countertop with flaxseed meal. Dust your hands as well.

4. Place the dough on your countertop. Fold the dough a few times to form into a ball. Place dough on a cotton cloth, with its seam side facing down. Sprinkle some cornstarch on top of the dough.

5. Wrap the dough lightly with the cloth and set aside for 2 hours to rise.

6. Preheat the oven to 450°F. Place a large greased loaf pan or Dutch oven in the oven while preheating.

7. Transfer the dough into the heated loaf pan carefully with its seam side facing up.

8. Cover with a lid or aluminum foil and bake for 40-50 minutes.

9. Uncover and continue baking for another 8-10 minutes. This is done to get a crust on top.

10. Turn off the oven and let the bread remain in the oven for 5 minutes.

11. Remove the bread from the oven and cool on a wire rack completely.

12. Slice and serve.

Quinoa Corn Cannabis Muffins

Serves: 20-25

Cooking time: 45 minutes

Ingredients:

- 1 cup quinoa, rinsed

- 2 cups water

- 2 cups whole-wheat pastry flour or canna-flour

- 1/2 teaspoon salt

- 1 cup light brown sugar or low-carb sweetener of your choice

- 1/2 cup cannabutter, melted

- 2 teaspoons vanilla extract

- 1 cup grilled or cooked corn (use only the kernels)

- 2 cups quinoa flour

- 2 teaspoons baking soda

- 2 eggs

- 2 1/2 cups plain yogurt

Method:

1. Preheat oven to 350°F.

2. To cook quinoa: Place a saucepan over medium heat. Add quinoa and water and stir.

3. When it starts to boil, lower the heat and cover with a lid. Cook

until dry.

4.   Turn off the heat and fluff using a fork. Cover and set aside
     for some time.

5.   Add flour, quinoa flour, salt, sugar and baking soda into a
     mixing bowl. Stir until well combined.

6.   Add eggs, yogurt, butter and vanilla into another bowl and
     whisk well. Pour into the mixture of dry ingredients. Stir until
     well combined and free from lumps.

7.   Grease 2 muffin tins of 12 counts each.

8.   Pour batter into the muffin tins. Fill up to 3/4. Bake in batches
     if required.

9.   Bake at 350°F for 25 minutes.

Breakfast Sandwiches

Serves: 4

Cooking time: 15 minutes

Ingredients:

- Salt to taste

- Pepper to taste

- 0.1-0.14 ounces cannabis, finely chopped

- 4 eggs, beaten

- 4 tablespoons butter

- 8 slices Velveeta cheese

- 8 slices bacon

- 8 slices bread

Method:

1. Place a nonstick skillet over low heat. Add bacon and cook until it becomes crisp. Remove with a slotted spoon and place on a plate that is lined with paper towels.

2. Whisk together eggs, salt, and pepper and pour the mixture in the skillet. Scramble and cook the eggs.

3. Butter the bread on one side only.

4. Take half the slices of bread. Sprinkle half the cannabis over them.

5. Place one cheese slice on each bread slice. Place a slice of bacon over the cheese. Divide and place the scrambled eggs

over them.

6. Place another slice of bacon over the scrambled eggs.

7. Place another cheese slice over the bacon. Sprinkle the remaining cannabis

8. Cover with the other 4 slices of bread, with the buttered side facing down. Press the sandwiches.

9. Place the sandwiches in a microwave and microwave for a few seconds until the cheese melts.

10. Chop into desired shape and serve.

Note: You can replace cannabis and butter with cannabutter

Cannabis Coffee Cake

Serves: 30-35

Cooking time: 20-30 minutes

Ingredients:

- 3/4 cup sugar

- 4 1/2 cups flour

- 2 eggs

- 1 1/3 cups milk

- 3/4 cup vegetable shortening

- 2 packages active yeast

- 2 eggs

- 3 tablespoons cannabutter, melted

- 1/2 teaspoon salt

Method:

1. Preheat oven to 375°F.

2. Grease a large baking pan or 2 smaller baking pans with cooking spray or some oil. Set aside.

3. Add 2 cups flour and yeast into a bowl and stir.

4. Place a saucepan over medium heat. Add milk, 1/2 cup sugar, and vegetable shortening.

5. Stir a couple of times. Turn the heat off when vegetable shortening becomes softer.

6. Transfer to the bowl of yeast and beat until well mixed.

7. Add eggs, one at a time, and beat well each time. Add remaining flour and mix until well combined. You will have malleable dough.

8. Transfer the dough to the baking pan. Scatter almonds on top. Sprinkle remaining sugar on top of the dough.

9. Cover the baking pan with a clean, moist cloth. Let it sit for around an hour. The dough should have risen by now.

10. Bake at 375°F for about 20 minutes.

11. Remove from the oven and cool.

12. Cut into slices and serve.

Café De Cannabis

Serves: 2

Cooking time: 5 minutes

Ingredients:

- 2 cups freshly brewed Cuban coffee

- 1/2 teaspoon ground cinnamon

- 2 good pinches Moroccan hash

- 2 tablespoons sugar

- 1/4 teaspoon ground nutmeg

Method:

1. Pour hot coffee into 2 cups.

2. Divide equally and add cinnamon, sugar, Moroccan hash, and nutmeg to the cups and stir.

3. Serve right away.

CHAPTER TWELVE

LUNCH RECIPES

Marijuana Avocado Shake

Serves: 1

Cooking Time: NA

Ingredients:

- 1/2 avocado, peeled, pitted, chopped

- Ice cubes, as required

- 1 1/2 tablespoons sugar or any other sweetener of your choice to taste

- 3/4 cup canna-milk

Method:

1. Add avocado, ice cubes, sugar, and canna-milk to a blender and blend well.

2. Pour into a tall glass and serve.

Banana and Strawberry Smoothie Infused with Cannabis

Ingredients:

- 1/4 cup orange juice

- 3/4 cup frozen strawberries

- 0.004 ounces hash oil or kief hash, decarbed

- 1/2 cup coconut milk

- 1 small banana, sliced, frozen

- 1/2 tablespoon hemp seeds (optional)

Method:

1. Add strawberries, kief hash, orange juice, banana, coconut milk, and hemp seeds (if using) to a blender.

2. Blend for 30-40 seconds or until smooth.

3. Pour into a tall glass and serve.

Cannabis Vegetable Tart

Serves: 4

Cooking time: 25 minutes

Ingredients:

- 1/2 frozen puff pastry sheet, thawed
- 1/2 leek, sliced
- 1 cup torn Swiss chard
- 1/4 teaspoon sweet paprika
- Salt to taste
- 3 tablespoons cannabutter
- 1/2 yellow bell pepper, chopped
- 2-4 tablespoons crumbled goat cheese
- 1/4 teaspoon cayenne pepper

Method:

1. Preheat oven to 350°F.
2. Take a baking sheet and place half a sheet of puff pastry over it.
3. Place a skillet over low heat. Add cannabutter. When butter melts, add leek and pepper and cook until slightly tender.
4. Stir in chard and cook for one minute. Turn the heat off.
5. Spoon the vegetables on the pastry sheet. Scatter goat cheese on top.

6. Bake at 350°F for 10-12 minutes or until the crust turns brown.

Smoked Mac 'n' Cheese

Serves: 2

Cooking time: 40 minutes

Ingredients:

- 2 cups milk

- 1/4 cup unsalted butter

- 1/4 cup cold cannabutter

- 1/2 tablespoon melted cannabutter

- 1/2 cup flour

- Salt and pepper, to taste

- 1/8 teaspoon cayenne pepper or to taste

- 1/2 cup smoked mozzarella cheese, grated

- 1/2 cup parmesan cheese, grated and divided

- 1/2 cup cheddar cheese, shredded

- 1/2 cup shredded American or Swiss cheese

- 2 tablespoons bread crumbs

Method

1. Preheat oven to 400°F.

2. Place a skillet over low heat. Add butter and cold cannabutter. When butter melts, stir in the flour and cook for 2-3 minutes until aromatic.

3. Meanwhile, heat milk. Turn off the heat when the milk is quite hot. Do not boil it.

4. Pour milk into the skillet, stirring constantly. Stir in the seasonings. Cook until thick, stirring all the while. When the mixture begins to boil, turn off the flame. Add pasta, smoked mozzarella, 6 tablespoons Parmesan, cheddar cheese, and American cheese. Mix well. Heat thoroughly and stir. Turn off the heat.

5. Transfer to a baking dish.

6. Bake at 400°F until the top is light brown.

7. Take out of the oven and cool for about 10 minutes and then serve.

Spinach Cannabis Quiche

Serves: 4

Cooking time: 30 minutes

Ingredients:

- 1/4 cup cannabutter

- 1/2 cup milk

- 1/2 small onion, finely chopped

- 2.25 ounces canned mushrooms, drained, chopped

- 4 ounces cheddar cheese, shredded

- Salt and pepper to taste

- 2 cloves garlic, finely minced

- 5 ounces frozen spinach, thawed, drained

- 3 ounces crumbled feta cheese

- 2 eggs, beaten

- 1 small (6 inch) deep pie crust, unbaked

Method:

1. Preheat oven to 400°F.

2. Place a skillet over low heat. Add cannabutter. When butter melts, add onion and garlic and sauté well.

3. Add mushroom and spinach and mix well. Cook for a couple of minutes until spinach wilts.

4. Stir in feta cheese and half the cheddar cheese. Add salt and pepper to taste. Mix well. Cook until cheese melts. Turn off the flame.

5. Spread this mixture over the pie crust.

6. Whisk together eggs and milk in a bowl. Pour the filling over the crust.

7. Bake at 400°F for 15 minutes or until the top is light brown.

8. Remove from the oven. Cool for about 10 minutes and then serve.

Weed Ramen Noodles

Serves: 2

Cooking time: 15 minutes

Ingredients:

- 2 servings ramen kimchi noodles

- 4 tablespoons butter

- -0.14 ounces weed, ground

- Hot chili sauce, to taste

- 1/2 cup cheese, grated

- 4 cups water

- teaspoon dried oregano

Method:

1. Place a pot over medium heat. Add water and weed. Heat, but don't allow to boil.

2. Add butter and simmer until the weed turns slightly brown in color. Do not boil. If it starts boiling, remove from heat and set aside for a while. Place it again over heat until it turns slightly brown in color.

3. Add the ramen noodles, kimchi, flavoring packet that comes with it, hot sauce, oregano, and cheese.

4. Simmer until the noodles are cooked.

5. Ladle into soup bowls and serve.

Marijuana Meatloaf

Serves: 10-12

Cooking time: 45-60 minutes

Ingredients:

- 2 large eggs

- 1/2 ounce cannabis

- 2 pounds ground beef or lamb or pork

- 1 package crushed saltines

- 1 cup green bell pepper, chopped

- 1 cup onion, chopped

- 1 cup melted cannabutter or canna-oil

- 1 1/2 teaspoons black pepper, powdered

- 2 cloves garlic, minced

- 1 1/2 teaspoon salt

Method

1. Preheat oven to 350°F.

2. Add meat, garlic, onion, and bell pepper to a large bowl and knead well.

3. Stir in saltines, cannabutter, and cannabis.

4. Transfer to a greased loaf pan. Spread evenly with a spatula.

5. Bake at 350°F for about 45-60 minutes.

6. Remove the loaf pan from oven. Set aside for a while to cool slightly.

7. Slice and serve.

Raspberry Pear Grilled Cheese Sandwich

Serves: 4

Cooking time: 20 minutes

Ingredients:

- 8 slices hearty whole-grain bread

- 2 ripe pears, peeled, cored, thinly sliced

- 4 tablespoons cannabutter, at room temperature

- 7-8 tablespoons raspberry jam or preserves

- 8 slices Muenster cheese

- Salt to taste

Method:

1. Place a large skillet over medium-high heat.

2. Spread 1/2 tablespoon butter on one side of a slice of bread. Spread 1 1/2-2 tablespoons jam on the other side of the bread slice.

3. Place the bread slice on the skillet, buttered side facing down.

4. Place a few pear slices over the jam side of the bread (the top). Place 2 slices of cheese over the pears. Lower the heat to low heat.

5. Cover the pan with a lid. Cook for a couple of minutes until cheese melts.

6. Spread butter on another slice of bread. Cover this slice over the sandwich, with the buttered side facing up.

7. Carefully lift the entire sandwich and flip sides. Cook until the underside is golden brown.

8. Remove to a plate. Cut into desired shape and serve.

9. Repeat steps 2-8 and make the remaining sandwiches.

Ham and Cheddar Panini

Serves: 4

Cooking time: 10 minutes

Ingredients:

- 4 rolls, split

- 1 pepper, cut into round slices

- 8 ounces ham, thinly sliced

- 2 tomatoes, thinly sliced

- 4 tablespoons canna-oil

- 8 ounces cheddar cheese, sliced

- Arugula leaves, as required

- 1 cup sauerkraut, drained

Method:

1. Place a skillet over low heat. Add oil and heat. Add pepper and cook until it becomes slightly tender. Take off the heat.

2. Place ham on the bottom half of the rolls. Divide the rest of the ingredients equally. Layer with arugula followed by tomatoes and cheese. Next layer with bell pepper slices and sauerkraut.

3. Cover with the top half of the rolls.

4. Grill in a preheated panini press until golden brown.

5. Remove from the press and cool for a couple of minutes. Cut into desired shape and serve.

Cannabis Mango-Cashew Fried Rice

Serves: 4

Cooking time: 30 minutes

Ingredients:

- 6 cups cooked brown rice, cold

- 1 cup raw cashew halves

- 2 tablespoons minced ginger

- 2 small Spanish onions, diced

- 1 cup frozen green peas, thawed

- 4 tablespoons low-sodium soy sauce

- 2 teaspoons Worcestershire sauce

- 1 teaspoon tarragon

- 1 teaspoon thyme

- Juice of 2 limes

- 2 mangoes, peeled, pitted, cut into ½ inch pieces

- 8 medium cloves garlic, peeled, minced

- 1 1/2 cups shiitake mushrooms, thinly sliced

- 2 large carrots, diced

- 6 tablespoons canna-extra-virgin olive oil

- 2 tablespoons sesame oil

- 1/2 teaspoon ground turmeric

- Salt to taste

- Pepper to taste

<u>Optional toppings:</u>

- Sesame seeds

- Chopped cilantro

- Sriracha sauce, etc.

Method:

1. Place an iron skillet over medium-low heat. Let the pan heat.

2. Add cashews and roast until light brown in color. Remove the cashews to a plate and set aside to cool.

3. Add 4 tablespoons canna-oil to the skillet and heat. When the oil is heated, add onion, ginger, carrots, and a pinch of salt and mix well. Cook until onions are pink.

4. Push the vegetables to one side of the skillet. Add 2 tablespoons canna-oil. Add half the rice in the center. Press the rice with a spatula. Let it cook for 2 minutes.

5. Now mix all the rice and vegetables in the skillet.

6. Add remaining rice, turmeric, tarragon, thyme, and toss well. Heat thoroughly.

7. Meanwhile, add sesame oil, Worcestershire sauce, and lime juice to a bowl and whisk well. Pour over the rice. Toss well.

8. Scatter peas, mangoes, and cashews and toss well.

9. Cook for 3-4 minutes, tossing frequently until peas and mango

pieces are warm and the rice is steaming hot.

10. Serve right away topped with optional toppings.

Vegan Cannabis Spaghetti Bolognese

Serves: 8

Cooking time: 20 minutes

Ingredients:

- 4 tablespoon vegan cannabutter or cannabutter if you are not vegan

- 16 ounces baby bella mushrooms

- 4 stalks celery, cut into pieces

- 4 carrots, scrubbed, cut into pieces

- 2 red onions, chopped

- 4 cloves garlic, peeled, minced

- 2 teaspoons crushed red pepper

- 2 tablespoons tomato paste

- 2 pounds pasta, cooked

- 2 tablespoons fennel seeds

- 2 cans whole, peeled plum tomatoes

- 2 teaspoons dried basil

- Salt to taste

- Pepper to taste

Method:

1. Add mushrooms to a food processor bowl. Process until finely

chopped.

2. Add carrots, onion, and celery to the food processor and process until finely chopped.

3. Place a large skillet over medium-high heat. Add vegan or normal cannabutter. When butter melts, add all the finely chopped vegetables and mushrooms and stir.

4. Add salt and pepper to taste. Saute until vegetables are cooked.

5. Stir in fennel seeds, garlic, and crushed red pepper. Cook for a minute or until aromatic.

6. Stir in tomato paste, tomatoes, salt, pepper, and basil. Mix well. Cook until the sauce is thick.

7. Serve over cooked pasta.

Weed Quesadillas

Serves: 4

Cooking time: minutes

Ingredients:

- 8 flour tortillas (6 inches each)

- 1 sweet bell pepper, chopped

- 1/2 cup chopped scallions

- 2 cups shredded mozzarella cheese

- 4 tablespoons cannabutter or canna-oil

- 8-12 raw shrimp, chopped

- Salt to taste

- Pepper to taste

- 1 teaspoon oregano or to taste

Method:

1. Place a pan over medium heat. Add canna-oil or butter and heat.

2. Stir in the peppers and cook until slightly tender.

3. Stir in the shrimp and cook for 1-2 minutes. Stir occasionally.

4. Stir in the scallions and cook for 2-3 minutes. Transfer to a bowl.

5. Add some more oil to the pan if required. Place a tortilla on the pan. Spread 1/4 of the filling on the tortilla. Sprinkle

cheese all over the filling.

6. Cover with another tortilla. Press the tortilla all over so that the ingredients stick to each other when cheese melts. Cook until the underside is browned to your liking.

7. Carefully flip sides of the quesadilla. Cook until the underside is browned to your liking.

8. Remove to a plate, cut into 4, and serve.

9. Repeat steps 5-8 and make the other quesadilla.

Laid-Back Latkes

Serves: 15-18

Cooking time: 30 minutes

Ingredients:

- 2 cups canna-vegetable oil

- 2 1/2 pounds Russet potatoes, unpeeled, grated

- 1 egg, beaten

- 1/2 teaspoon salt or to taste

- 1 cup cooked rice or couscous or any other grain of your choice

- 1 onion, grated

- 1/4 cup flour or more if required

- Ground pepper, to taste

Method:

1. Place grated potatoes in a bowl of water for a while.

2. Drain the potatoes and place in a colander. Press the potatoes against the colander to remove excess water.

3. Add potatoes, onion, egg, salt, and pepper into a bowl. Mix well. If the mixture is too watery, add some more flour.

4. Place a large pan over medium-high heat. Add canna-vegetable oil and heat. The oil should be well heated but not smoking.

5. Scoop about a heaping tablespoon of pancake mixture into the pan. Flatten to shape into pancake. Place as many as can fit in

the pan. Cook until underside is golden brown. Flip sides and cook the other side until it turns golden brown.

6. Remove with a slotted spoon and place on a bed of rice.

7. Repeat with the remaining batter. Serve with sour cream.

CHAPTER THIRTEEN

Baked Shrimp Scampi

Serves: 3

Cooking time: minutes

Ingredients:

- 1 pound shrimp in shell, peeled, deveined, leave the tails, butterflied

- 1 tablespoon dry white wine

- 6 tablespoons cannabutter, at room temperature

- 2 tablespoons minced shallots

- 1/2 teaspoon minced fresh rosemary leaves

- 1 1/2 tablespoons minced fresh parsley

- 1/8 teaspoon crushed red pepper flakes

- 1 tablespoon fresh lemon juice

- 1/3 cup panko bread crumbs

- 1 1/2 tablespoons canna-oil

- Kosher salt to taste

- Pepper to taste

- 2 teaspoons minced garlic

- 1/2 teaspoon grated lemon zest

- Yolk of a medium egg

- Lemon wedges for garnish

Method:

1. Preheat oven to 350°F.

2. Add shrimp to a bowl. Pour wine and oil over it. Sprinkle salt and pepper to taste. Toss well. Set aside for 10 minutes.

3. Add garlic, red pepper flakes, shallots, herbs, butter, lemon juice, lemon zest, panko bread crumbs, yolk, salt, and pepper to a bowl and mix well.

4. Take a small oval dish of about 9-10 inches. Place shrimp on the bottom of the dish, with the curled tail side facing up. Place them in a single layer.

5. Spoon the bread-crumb mixture over the shrimp.

6. Bake at 350°F for about 10-12 minutes or until the mixture is bubbling.

7. For a brown top, broil for a minute.

8. Let cool for a couple of minutes before serving. Garnish with lemon wedges and serve.

Broccoli Cheddar Casserole

Serves: 6-8

Cooking time: 50-60 minutes

Ingredients:

- 30 ounces broccoli, chopped into florets

- 1 1/2 cans cream of mushroom soup

- 3 eggs, beaten

- 6 tablespoons cannabutter

- 1 1/2 cups mayonnaise

- 1 1/2 cups grated sharp cheddar cheese

- 3 cups crushed crackers

Method:

1. Preheat oven to 350°F.

2. Place a pot half filled with water over medium heat. Bring to a boil.

3. Add broccoli and cook until the color changes to bright green.

4. Drain and immerse broccoli in bowl of iced water. Drain after 3 minutes.

5. Place broccoli in a bowl. Add mayonnaise, cheddar cheese, soup, and eggs. Mix well.

6. Grease a casserole dish or baking dish with some oil.

7. Spread the broccoli mixture in the prepared baking dish.

8. Sprinkle crackers over the broccoli layer.

9. Melt butter and pour all over the crackers.

10. Bake at 350°F for about 30-40 minutes or until it turns golden brown.

11. Take it off the oven and cool for 5 minutes.

12. Serve.

Cannabis-Infused Turkey Bolognese

Serves: 3-4

Cooking time: 30 minutes

Ingredients:

- 1/2 box whole-wheat spaghetti

- 1/2 pound ground turkey

- 1/2 can (from a 7.2 ounce can) tomato sauce

- 1 medium onion, finely chopped

- 2 cloves garlic, peeled, minced

- 1/2 cup grated parmesan cheese

- 4-6 drops cannabis tincture

- 1 tablespoon olive oil

- 1/2 can (from a 28 ounce can) chopped tomatoes

- 2 medium carrots, finely chopped

- 1 stalk celery, finely chopped

- 2 tablespoons chopped parsley

- Salt and pepper, to taste

Method:

1. Place a skillet over medium heat and add some oil. When the oil is heated, add carrots, onion, and celery and stir. Cook the vegetables well.

2. Stir in the ground turkey and garlic and cook until they turn brown.

3. Stir in the tomato sauce and diced tomatoes.

4. Meanwhile, cook spaghetti following the instructions on the package. Drain, retaining 3-4 tablespoons of cooked water.

5. Toss together spaghetti and cannabis tincture and add into the pot. Add the retained water and turkey mixture. Mix well.

6. Garnish with parsley and cheese and serve.

Rasta Pasta

Serves: 4-6

Cooking time: 30 minutes

Ingredients:

- 4 cups shell pasta

- 1 bell pepper of any color, cut into 1/2-inch squares

- 2 cloves garlic, peeled, sliced

- 8 tablespoons flour

- 2-3 teaspoons chopped, fresh dill

- 1 tablespoon soy sauce or to taste

- 3/4 cup canna-milk

- 1 onion, chopped

- 4 tablespoons margarine or canna-margarine

- 1 teaspoon wet mustard

- 6 tablespoons nutritional yeast

Method:

1. Cook pasta following the directions on the package. Drain and set aside.

2. Place a pan over medium-low heat. Add 1 tablespoon margarine and melt.

3. Add onion, bell pepper, and garlic and sauté until onion turns translucent. Transfer to the bowl of pasta.

4. Place the saucepan back over heat. Add remaining margarine and melt.

5. Add flour and stir for about a minute. Add canna-milk and stir constantly until well combined. Continue stirring until the sauce thickens.

6. Add in the pasta and vegetables and mix. Heat thoroughly.

7. Serve hot.

Rib Eye with Chimichurri Sauce

Serves: 10

Cooking time: 10 minutes

Ingredients:

<u>For chimichurri sauce:</u>

- 1 cup chopped parsley

- 1/2 tablespoon red wine vinegar

- 3-4 tablespoons chopped parsley

- 4 cannabis fan leaves, finely chopped

- 1/2 teaspoon red chili flakes

- 1 cup canola oil or neutral oil

- 1 teaspoon oregano

- 1/2 tablespoon salt

- 1 cup olive oil

<u>For rib eye:</u>

- 1 bone-in rib-eye steak

- 1 tablespoon kief-infused butter (optional)

- Salt to taste

- Pepper, to taste

- 7-8 tablespoons olive oil

Method:

1. To make chimichurri sauce: Add parsley, salt, vinegar, red chili flakes, cannabis leaves, garlic, oregano, olive oil, and canola oil to a large bowl.

2. Sprinkle salt and pepper generously over the steak. Rub well into the steak. Place steak in a bowl. Do not cover the bowl. Chill for 8-10 hours.

3. Remove steak from the refrigerator and bring to room temperature before cooking.

4. Place a cast iron pan over medium heat. Add oil and heat. Place rib-eye steak in the pan and cook until underside is brown. Flip sides and cook the other side until brown and cooked to liking. It should take approximately 8-10 minutes for medium-rare.

5. Remove steak and place on your cutting board. Let sit for 10 minutes.

6. Slice the steak to desired size

7. Serve steak slices with chimichurri sauce.

Chicken Pic-Canna

Serves: 2

Cooking time: 15 minutes

Ingredients:

- 1 chicken breast, boneless, pounded, halved

- 2 tablespoons canna-oil

- 3-4 tablespoons cannabutter

- 1/4 cup lemon juice

- 3-4 tablespoons capers

- Salt and pepper to taste

- 1/4 cup chicken stock

- 2 tablespoons chopped parsley

- 1/2 cup all-purpose flour

Method:

1. Season the chicken with salt and pepper

2. Place flour on a plate. Coat the chicken all over with flour.

3. Place a pan over medium heat. Add 1 tablespoon cannabutter and 1 1/2 tablespoons canna-oil and heat.

4. Place chicken in the pan and roast for 2-3 minutes. Flip sides and cook the other side for 2-3 minutes. Remove chicken to a plate.

5. Add stock, capers, and lemon juice into the same pan. Place

pan over medium heat. When the mixture is hot, add chicken and cook for 4-5 minutes.

6. Remove chicken with a slotted spoon and place on a plate.

7. Add 1 tablespoon canna-oil and remaining cannabutter to the pan. Whisk until butter melts and is well incorporated into the sauce.

8. Spoon the sauce over the chicken. Sprinkle parsley on top and serve.

Chicken Pot-cciatore

Serves: 8

Cooking time: 20-25 minutes

Ingredients:

- 2 fryer chickens, with skin, cut into pieces
- 2 tablespoons cannabutter
- 2 tablespoons olive oil
- 1 cup white wine (optional)
- 5-6 green olives, sliced
- 5-6 black olives, sliced
- Salt and pepper, as per taste
- 2 large onions, cut into 1/2-inch wedges
- 2 cups small cremini mushrooms

Method:

1. Dry the chicken after rinsing by patting with paper towels.

2. Season the chicken.

3. Place a skillet over medium heat and warm the oil and butter.

4. Add chicken pieces in batches and cook until brown. Remove with a slotted spoon and place on a plate lined with paper towels.

5. Add onions into the same pan and cook well.

6. Lower the heat and add the browned chicken back into the pan. Also add mushrooms and cook for 4-5 minutes.

7. Stir in wine and simmer for a couple of minutes. Add olives and mix well. Take off heat; cover and set aside for a few minutes before serving.

Cannabis Chicken Pot Pie

Serves: 8

Cooking time: 45-50 minutes

Ingredients:

- 2 pounds chicken breasts halves, boneless, skinless, chopped into cubes
- 2 cups frozen green peas
- 2 cups carrots, sliced
- 1 large onion, shopped
- 1 stalk celery, sliced
- 2/3 cup cannabutter
- 1 1/3 cups canna-milk
- 2/3 cup all-purpose flour
- 3 1/2 cups chicken broth
- 1/8 teaspoon celery seeds
- Salt to taste
- Pepper to taste
- 4 unbaked pie crusts (9 inches each)
- Water as required

Method:

1. Preheat oven to 425°F.

2. Add chicken, peas, carrots, and celery into a saucepan. Place the saucepan over medium heat.

3. Pour enough water to just cover the ingredients in the saucepan.

4. When it begins to boil, cook for about 15 minutes. Remove from heat. Drain the water and put the chicken and vegetables aside.

5. Place a saucepan over medium heat. Add cannabutter. When the butter melts, add onions and sauté until translucent.

6. Add flour, salt, pepper, and celery seeds and sauté for a minute or so until aromatic.

7. Pour the canna-milk and chicken broth slowly, stirring simultaneously.

8. Lower heat and simmer until thick. Turn off the heat.

9. Take 2 of the pie crusts. Divide and keep the chicken and vegetable mixture on it. Spread it all over the crust.

10. Pour the chicken broth mix over it.

11. Cover with the remaining 2 pie crusts. Press the edges of both the crusts together and seal all around.

12. Using a sharp knife, make a few slits on the top crust.

13. Bake at 425°F until the top becomes golden.

14. Remove from the oven and cool.

15. Serve.

Gnocchi in Ganja Butter

Serves: 2

Cooking time: 30-40 minutes

Ingredients:

- 3 medium baking potatoes, skin on, rinsed

- 1 small egg, slightly beaten

- 1 1/2 cups flour or more if required

- 1 tablespoon cannabutter

- 1/2 tablespoon plain olive oil

- 1/2 teaspoon baking powder

- Salt to taste

<u>To serve:</u>

- Grated parmesan cheese or Romano cheese or Asiago cheese, to garnish (optional)

- 2 cloves garlic, minced

- 1 tablespoon cannabutter

- 1/2 tablespoon olive oil or coconut oil

- Red sauce (optional)

Method:

1. Place a pot of water with potatoes and a little salt over medium heat. Boil until the potatoes are cooked.

2. Peel the potatoes and pass through a sieve so that the potatoes are well mashed and free of lumps. Alternately, mash the

potatoes using a potato masher until smooth and free of lumps.

3. Add potatoes, egg, flour, cannabutter, olive oil, baking powder, and salt into a bowl. Mix until well combined and dough is formed. The dough will be bread-dough-like to look at.

4. Take a portion of the dough (cover the remaining dough with a cotton cloth). Roll it between your hands until it is about 5-6 inches long and about an inch in width. Then cut into about 1-1 1/2 inch pieces.

5. Press the pieces with the prongs of the fork to create ridges on the gnocchi.

6. Dust a baking sheet with some flour. Place the cut gnocchi over the baking sheet. Dust the top of the gnocchi with a little flour. Cover with a cotton cloth until ready to use. They may turn slightly gray but that doesn't matter, as they will turn white again after boiling.

7. To boil, place a pot of water over medium heat. Add 1-2 teaspoons salt and 1 tablespoon olive oil.

8. When the water boils, put the gnocchi in the water. Slowly the gnocchi will rise to the top. After it rises, let it boil for 5 minutes.

9. Drain in a colander. Rise **under** until hot water. Transfer to a bowl.

10. To serve: Place a small pan over medium heat. Add canna-butter and olive oil to the pan. When the butter melts, add garlic and cook until brown.

11. Pour over the gnocchi. Drizzle red sauce over it. Sprinkle cheese on top and serve.

Dope Dumplings Vegetable Casserole

Serves: 2-3

Cooking time: 80-90 minutes

Ingredients:

<u>For veggie casserole:</u>

- 4 ounces parsnips, peeled, sliced

- 1 stick celery, sliced

- 1 ounce butter

- 1/2 can baked beans

- 1/2 ounce flour

- 1/4 cup white wine

- 1/2 teaspoon mixed dried herbs

- 2 carrots, sliced

- 1/2 leek, sliced

- 1 medium onion, chopped

- 1 small clove garlic, crushed

- 1 cup stock

- 3.5 ounces button mushrooms, chopped

- Salt to taste

- Pepper to taste

<u>For dope dumplings:</u>

- 2 ounces self-rising flour

- 1/2 teaspoon mustard powder

- 1/2 ounce butter

- 1 ounce grated cheese

- 1/16 ounce ground cannabis

Method:

1. Place a pan over medium heat. Add butter. When butter melts, add onion and garlic and cook until translucent.

2. Add flour and stir constantly for a couple of minutes. Turn off the heat.

3. Stir in wine and stock.

4. Add rest of the ingredients for casserole and mix well. Transfer to a casserole dish.

5. Place casserole dish over low heat. Cover with lid and cook for 40-50 minutes. Stir occasionally.

6. Meanwhile, make the dumplings as follows: Mix together in a bowl, mustard, flour, and cannabis. Add butter and rub into the mixture. Add cheese and mix well.

7. Sprinkle some water and mix until soft dough is formed.

8. Divide the dough into 5-6 equal portions and shape into balls.

9. Place the dumplings on top of the veggie mixture in the casserole. Cover and continue cooking for another 20-25 minutes.

10. Serve hot.

Classic Cannabis Lasagna

Serves: 3-4

Cooking time: 50-60 minutes

Ingredients:

- 1/2 pound ground turkey or beef

- 1 small onion, finely chopped

- 1/2 can (from a 14.5 ounces can) stewed tomatoes

- 1/2 can (from a 6 ounces can) tomato paste

- 1/2 jar (from a 6 ounce jar) tomato sauce

- 1 large egg

- 1/4 cup ricotta cheese

- 1 teaspoon chopped fresh parsley

- 1/2 teaspoon pepper or to taste

- 4 ounces shredded cheddar cheese

- 4 ounces shredded mozzarella cheese

- 4 ounces grated parmesan cheese

- 3/4 cup cottage cheese

- 1 teaspoon salt

- 1/2 box (from a 8 ounces bag) no-boil lasagna noodles

- 1 clove garlic, minced

- 1 1/2 tablespoons canna-extra-virgin olive oil

Method:

1. Preheat oven to 350°F.

2. Grease a square or rectangular baking dish with some oil.

3. Place a skillet over medium-low heat. Add canna-oil and heat but do not let the oil smoke.

4. Add garlic and onion and sauté for a minute. Add 1/2 teaspoon salt and 1/4 teaspoon pepper. Mix well.

5. Add turkey and cook until brown. Break up the meat as it cooks. Remove any excess fat from the pan.

6. Add tomato sauce, stewed tomatoes, and tomato paste and stir. Cover and continue cooking for 10-12 minutes. Stir every 5 minutes.

7. Add egg into a bowl and whisk well. Add 3/4 cup cottage cheese, 1/4 cup Parmesan cheese, 1/4 cup ricotta cheese, 1 teaspoon chopped parsley, 1/2 teaspoon salt, and 1/4 teaspoon pepper and mix until well incorporated.

8. Add a thin layer of turkey sauce on the bottom of the baking dish.

9. Place a layer of lasagna noodles, slightly overlapping.

10. Spread half the cottage cheese mixture over the noodles followed by half the remaining mozzarella and half the cheddar cheese. Spread some turkey sauce over this layer.

11. Repeat steps 8-9.

12. Sprinkle remaining Parmesan cheese on top.

13. Bake at 350°F for about 25-30 minutes or until thoroughly

heated.

Pesto Cannabis Pizza

Serves: 2

Cooking time: 30 minutes

Ingredients:

<u>For pesto:</u>

- 1/2 cup canna-oil

- 1 clove garlic, peeled

- Salt to taste

- 1 cup fresh basil

- 2 tablespoons parmesan cheese, grated

<u>For pizza:</u>

- Pizza dough for 1 small pizza, rolled, or use a pre-cooked pizza base

- 1/4 cup goat cheese, crumbled

- 1/2 small red pepper, diced

- 1 small tomato, sliced

- 1/4 cup shredded mozzarella cheese

Method:

1. Preheat oven to 200°F.

2. Add all the ingredients for pesto into a blender and blend until smooth.

3. Spread the pesto over the pizza dough.

4. Place red pepper and tomato slices over the pizza.

5. Sprinkle goat cheese and mozzarella cheese.

6. Bake at 200-220°F for about 25-30 minutes. Do not raise the heat, as cannabis will evaporate.

7. Cut into wedges and serve.

Cannabis Mashed Potatoes

Serves: 3

Cooking time: 25 minutes

Ingredients:

- 1 1/2 pounds russet potatoes, peeled, cut into small cubes

- 4 tablespoons cannabutter + extra to serve

- Kosher salt to taste

- Freshly ground pepper, as per taste

- 1/4 cup canna-milk

- 1 1/2 tablespoons horseradish

- 1/2 cup sour cream

- Chopped chives, to garnish

Method:

1. Add water to a pot and place the pot over medium heat.

2. Add potatoes and about a teaspoon of salt. Cook until the potatoes are tender.

3. Drain the potatoes and discard the water. Add the potatoes back to the pot. Mash with a potato masher.

4. Add cannabutter and milk to a small saucepan. Place over medium heat. When the mixture is warm, turn off the heat. Pour into the pot.Add salt and pepper. Mix well.

5. Garnish with chives and serve.

Chicken and Vegetables Thai Curry

Serves: 4-5

Cooking time: 40-45 minutes

Ingredients:

- 4-5 tablespoons canna-coconut oil

- 2 cans coconut milk

- 1 medium eggplant, cut into small pieces

- 5 new potatoes, halved

- Cooked basmati rice, to serve

- 4-5 chicken thighs, boneless, skinless, chopped into chunks

- 1 small cauliflower, cut into florets

- 3-4 tablespoons curry paste or to taste

- 3 tablespoons toasted, flaked coconut

Method:

1. Preheat oven to 400°F.

2. Spread eggplant, potatoes, and cauliflower on a greased baking sheet.

3. Roast at 400°F for about 20 minutes.

4. Place a pot over medium flame. Add canna-coconut oil. When the oil is heated, add chicken and cook until brown.

5. Add the roasted vegetables, curry paste, and coconut milk and mix well. Cook until chicken is done. Stir a couple of times

while it is cooking.

6. Garnish with toasted coconut. Serve over rice.

Cannabis Tuna Steaks with Sautéed Spinach

Serves: 4

Cooking time: 25 minutes

Ingredients:

<u>For tuna steaks:</u>

- 4 tuna steaks or ahi or yellowfin steaks (4 ounces each), rinsed

- 4 tablespoons low-sodium soy sauce

- Juice of 2 limes

- 2 teaspoons chopped fresh dill

- Salt and pepper, as per taste

- 3-4 tablespoons canna-extra-virgin olive oil

- 4 cloves garlic, peeled, finely minced

- 2 tablespoons honey

- 2 teaspoons finely minced fresh ginger

<u>For sautéed vegetables:</u>

- 2 tablespoons canna-extra-virgin olive oil

- 2 small white onions, finely diced

- 8 cups baby spinach

- 2 yellow bell peppers, deseeded, finely diced

- 8 cloves garlic, peeled, finely minced

- Salt and pepper, as per taste

Method:

1. Dry the tuna steaks by patting with paper towels. Sprinkle salt and pepper on either side of the steaks.

2. Brush canna-oil over the steaks. Place on a plate and set aside.

3. Take a wide bowl. Add remaining oil, lime juice, soy sauce, garlic, dill, ginger, and honey and mix well.

4. Place steak in this mixture. Coat well on either side. Place the bowl in the refrigerator for 2-3 hours.

5. Place a skillet over medium heat. Add 2 tablespoons canna-oil. When the oil is heated, add onion, bell pepper, salt, and pepper and sauté until onions are pink.

6. Stir in the baby spinach and stir. Cook until spinach wilts. Transfer to a serving platter and set aside.

7. Add remaining oil to the skillet and let heat.

8. Remove steaks from the marinade and place in the skillet. Cook for 4-5 minutes. Flip sides and cook the other side for 4-5 minutes or until the steak is cooked medium-rare to rare.

9. Remove with a slotted spoon and place over the cooked vegetables.

10. You can also add the marinade to a saucepan and place over medium heat. Simmer until thick. Spoon this sauce over the steak and serve.

Lobster Étouffée

Serves: 4

Cooking time: 45 minutes

Ingredients:

- 2 tablespoons oil

- 1/4 teaspoon cannabutter

- 1/4 cup regular butter, divided

- 1/4 cup flour + extra to make paste

- 2 cloves, peeled, minced

- 1/4 teaspoon white pepper

- 1/4 teaspoon black pepper

- 1/2 teaspoon Cajun seasoning

- 2 cups lobster stock

- 1/2 teaspoon salt

- 2 scallions, sliced + extra to garnish

- 1/4 cup green bell pepper, chopped

- 3/4 cup yellow onion, chopped

- 1 bay leaf

- 1/2 can (from a 14.5 ounce can) diced tomatoes

- 2 lobster tails, halved

- 1/4 cup fresh parsley, chopped

- Hot sauce to taste

- Hot cooked rice, to serve

Method:

1. Place a heavy saucepan over low heat. Add 2 tablespoons regular butter and cannabutter. When it melts, add flour and mix well. Stir constantly until aromatic.

2. Stir in the onion, garlic, and green pepper and cook well.

3. Stir in the lobster stock, tomatoes with juice, black pepper, white pepper, Cajun seasoning, hot sauce, parsley, scallion, salt, and cayenne pepper. Mix well.

4. Bring to a boil, stirring constantly. Lower the heat and simmer until thick.

5. Add lobster and simmer for 5 minutes.

6. Turn off the heat. Add 2 tablespoons regular butter and stir until it melts.

7. Sprinkle scallions and parsley and serve over rice.

Cannabis Fish Tacos

Serves: 8

Cooking time: 6 minutes

Ingredients:

- 4 cups sliced green cabbage

- 1 1/2 pounds white-fish fillets

- 1/4 teaspoon salt or to taste

- 2 tablespoons canna-oil

- 1/4 cup salsa

- 1/2 jalapeño, diced

- 1 onion, diced

- 8 corn tortillas

- Lime wedges, to garnish

- 4 teaspoons fajita seasoning

- 2 tablespoons lime juice

- 6 tablespoons chopped fresh cilantro

- 2 tomatoes, diced

- 1 small avocado, peeled, pitted, chopped

Method:

1. Place a pan over medium heat. Spray with cooking spray.

2. Sprinkle fajita seasoning on either side of the fish and rub gently into the fish.

3. Place on a preheated grill and grill for 3 minutes. Flip sides and grill for 3 minutes.

4. Remove from the grill and place on cutting board. Flake the fish into pieces using a fork. Set aside and keep warm in an oven.

5. Add cabbage, salt, lime juice, and cilantro to a bowl. Mix well and set aside. Add canna-oil, onion, tomato, jalapeños, and salsa to a bowl. Mix well.

6. Follow the instructions on the package of the tortillas and warm them.

7. Place tortillas on your countertop. Divide the fish among the tortillas. Divide the salsa mixture among the tortillas. Divide the cabbage mixture among the tortillas.

8. Scatter avocado slices on top.

9. Serve with lime wedges.

CHAPTER FOURTEEN

SOUP AND SALAD RECIPES

Pumpkin Potato Soup

Serves: 4-6

Cooking time: 25 minutes

Ingredients:

- 8 white potatoes, peeled, chopped

- 6 large carrots, sliced

- 2 medium red onions, chopped

- 6 stalks celery, sliced

- 10 cloves garlic, peeled, minced

- 4 cups pumpkin puree

- 8 cups vegetable broth

- 1 teaspoon ground nutmeg

- 4 tablespoons canna-coconut oil

- 2 cups coconut milk

- 2 teaspoons ground cinnamon

- Salt to taste

- Pepper to taste

<u>Optional toppings:</u>

- Pumpkin seeds

- A handful fresh sage, chopped

- Any other toppings of your choice

Method:

1. Place a large Dutch oven or soup pot over medium flame. Add canna-coconut oil. When the oil melts, add onion and potato and sauté for 5 minutes. Stir once during this time.

2. Stir in carrots and celery.

3. Add garlic, salt, and pepper and sauté until aromatic.

4. Stir in pumpkin, broth, coconut milk, and nutmeg.

5. Raise the heat to medium-high heat. When the mixture begins to boil, lower the heat to low and cook until potatoes are soft. Turn off the heat.

6. Blend with an immersion blender until you achieve the consistency you desire.

7. Ladle into soup bowls and serve.

Fresh Tomato Soup

Serves: 3-4

Cooking Time: NA

Ingredients:

- 1 1/2 pounds tomatoes, chopped into chunks

- 1 large clove garlic, peeled, minced

- 1 small red onion, quartered

- Pepper to taste

- Coarse salt to taste

- 1 1/2 tablespoons canna-oil

- 1 teaspoon lemon juice

- 1 1/2 tablespoons balsamic vinegar

To garnish:

- 1 tablespoon feta cheese, crumbled

- 2 tablespoons chopped parsley

Method:

1. Add tomatoes, garlic, salt, pepper, and lemon juice to a bowl and toss well. Cover and set aside for a while to allow the flavors to mingle.

2. Transfer to a blender. Add onion and vinegar and blend until the texture you desire is achieved. Transfer to a bowl. Cover and place in the refrigerator until ready to use.

3. Ladle into soup bowls. Garnish with feta and parsley and serve.

Cannabis Quinoa Stew

Serves: 8

Cooking time: 30 minutes

Ingredients:

- 1 cup quinoa, rinsed, drained
- 4 cups chopped onions
- 2 cups chopped bell peppers
- 2 cups chopped potatoes
- 3 cups chopped tomatoes
- 2 cups diced zucchini
- 1/2 cup scallions
- 1/2 cup canna-oil
- 2 teaspoons ground coriander
- 2 teaspoons dried oregano
- 2 teaspoons ground cumin
- 6 cups vegetable stock
- 2 tablespoons lemon juice
- 2 teaspoons sea salt or to taste
- 1 teaspoon pepper or to taste

Method:

1. Place a large saucepan or soup pot over medium heat. Add canna-oil and heat. When the oil is heated, add onion and a bit of salt and cook until translucent.

2. Stir in quinoa, bell pepper, zucchini, bell peppers, tomatoes, spices, and stock and mix well. Cover with a lid.

3. When the mixture boils, reduce the heat and cook the vegetables until they are tender.

4. Ladle into soup bowls. Sprinkle scallions on top and serve.

Chili Con Cannabis

Serves: 12-15

Cooking time: 2 1/2 hours

Ingredients:

- 3 cans (15 ounces each) black beans, drained
- 3 cans (15 ounces each) dark red kidney beans, drained
- 3 cans (15 ounce each) black-eyed peas, drained
- 3 medium sweet onions, chopped
- 1/2 cup dry red wine
- 2-3 tablespoons ground cumin
- 2-3 tablespoons dried New Mexico chili flakes
- 2-3 pounds chopped beef (the stir-fry type)
- 3 tablespoons chili powder
- 4-5 tablespoons Lea and Perrins sauce
- 4-5 tablespoons cannabutter
- 1 tablespoon canna-extra-virgin olive oil
- 10-12 cloves garlic, peeled, sliced

Method:

1. Add all the beans to a large pot. Place pot over low heat. When the beans are well heated, add wine, Lea and Perrins sauce, liquid smoke, cumin, chili powder, and chili flakes.

2. Cover with a lid. Let simmer for about an hour. Stir occasionally.

3. Stir in the onions and tomatoes.

4. Place a skillet over medium heat. Heat oil. Add garlic and fry it well.

5. Add beef and cook until brown. Transfer into the pot. Mix well.

6. Put a lid on the pot and cook on low heat for about 1-1 1/2 hours, stirring occasionally.

7. Add cannabutter and simmer for 25 minutes.

8. Serve in bowls.

Split Pea and Carrot Soup

http://www.weedist.com/2014/09/great-edibles-recipes-medicated-vegan-split-pea-soup/http://www.weedist.com/2014/09/great-edibles-recipes-medicated-vegan-split-pea-soup/

Serves: 3-4

Cooking time: minutes

Ingredients:

- 2 cups dried split peas, rinsed

- 2-2 1/2 cups water

- 2 1/2 cups vegetable broth

- 4 cloves garlic, peeled, minced

- 1 1/2 tablespoon canna-coconut oil

- 1 carrot, cut into bite-size pieces

- 1/2 tablespoon canna-extra-virgin olive oil

- 1 medium onion, finely diced

- 1 1/2-2 tablespoons white miso paste

- 1/2 teaspoon thyme

- Salt and pepper, as per taste

- 1 bay leaf

Method:

1. Place a Dutch oven or soup pot over medium heat. Add canna-extra-virgin olive oil. When the oil is heated, add onion and

garlic and cook until onions are translucent.

2. Add carrot and split peas. Season with salt and pepper.

3. Add miso, thyme, canna-coconut oil, and bay leaf and mix well.

4. Stir in broth and water.

5. When mixture begins to boil, lower the heat and cover with a lid. Simmer until split peas are cooked. Stir every 10-12 minutes.

6. Ladle into soup bowls and serve.

Butternut Squash Soup

Serves: 3

Cooking time: 20 minutes

Ingredients:

- 1 tablespoon chopped parsley

- 1/2 tablespoon chopped sage leaves

- 1/2 teaspoon chopped thyme

- 3/4 tablespoon canna-oil or cannabutter

- 3/4 tablespoon cannabutter, to finish

- 1/2 cup celery, chopped

- 1 1/2 pounds butternut squash, peeled, deseeded, chopped

- 1 carrot, chopped

- 1 onion, minced

- 3 teaspoons mild curry powder

- Salt and pepper to taste

- 2 1/2 cups vegetable stock

Method

1. Place a pan over medium flame. Add canna-oil. When the oil is hot, add onions and cook them.

2. Add rest of the ingredients except cannabutter and cook until the vegetables are soft.

3. When done, blend with an immersion blender until smooth. Taste and adjust the seasonings if necessary

4. Ladle into soup bowls. Add 1/4 tablespoon butter to each bowl.

5. Stir and serve hot.

Medicated French Onion Soup

Serves: 3

Cooking time: 50-60 minutes

Ingredients:

- 1 bay leaf

- 1/2 teaspoon pepper

- 2-3 sprigs thyme

- 3 large Spanish onions, halved, thinly sliced

- 2 tablespoons butter

- 2 tablespoons cannabutter

- 1/4 cup red wine

- 4 cups unsalted beef broth or water

- 1 teaspoon kosher salt

- 1 cup shredded gruyere cheese

- 1/2 French bread baguette, sliced, toasted

- Oyster crackers to serve

Method:

1. Place a soup pot over medium-low heat. Add butter and cannabutter. When it melts, add onions and cook on low until golden brown. Stir every 4-5 minutes. It can take a while to caramelize.

2. Meanwhile, toast the baguette slices on both sides and set

aside.

3. Add broth, water, red wine, pepper, and salt into the pot after the onions are caramelized. Mix well.

4. Simmer for about 15 minutes.

5. Set the oven to broiler mode.

6. Take 3 ovenproof bowls. Place a slice of toasted bread in each bowl. Place the bowls on a baking sheet.

7. Pour soup into the bowls. Sprinkle cheese on top.

8. Broil in a preheated oven at 150 degrees F until cheese melts and is browned to your liking.

9. Garnish with a sprig of thyme in each bowl and serve.

Cannabis Chicken Noodle Soup

Serves: 8

Cooking time: 30 minutes

Ingredients:

- 1 pound chicken, diced, cooked
- 8 cups chicken broth
- 1 cup chopped carrots
- 2 celery stalks, diced
- 1/2 cup frozen peas, thawed
- 1 cup chopped onions
- Salt to taste
- Pepper to taste
- 12 drops cannabis tincture
- 2 tablespoons butter
- 2 cups vegetable broth
- 1 teaspoon oregano
- 1 teaspoon basil
- 3 cups egg noodles

Method:

1. Place a pot over medium flame.

2. Add butter and let melt. When the butter melts, add onions, carrots, and celery and cook well. Stir occasionally.

3. Add chicken, oregano, basil, noodles, peas, cannabis tincture, and chicken stock.

4. Cover the pot and cook until the noodles and veggies are tender.

5. Add salt and pepper and stir.

6. Ladle into soup bowls and serve hot.

Cannabis Cabbage Salad with Sesame-Lime Dressing

Serves: 1-2

Cooking Time: NA

<u>For salad:</u>

- 6 ounces shredded cabbage

- 1/2 cup shredded carrots

- 1 small cucumber, cut into thin strips

- 1/2 tablespoon fresh chopped dill

- 1/2 Granny Smith apple, cored, cut into thin strips

- 1 small red onion, thinly sliced

- 1 tablespoon chives, chopped

- 3 tablespoons walnuts, chopped

<u>For sesame lime dressing:</u>

- 1/4 cup fresh lime juice

- 1 tablespoon honey

- 1/8 teaspoon minced ginger

- 1 1/2 tablespoon canna-extra-virgin olive oil

- 1 tablespoon diced shallots

- 1/2 teaspoon sesame oil

- 1/2 tablespoon apple cider vinegar

- 1 clove garlic, peeled, minced

- 1/2 tablespoon low-sodium soy sauce

- Salt to taste

- Pepper to taste

Method:

1. Add all the ingredients for dressing into a jar. Shake the jar vigorously until well combined. Set aside for a while to allow the flavors to mingle.

2. Add all the ingredients for salad into a bowl and toss well.

3. Pour dressing on top of salad. Toss well and serve.

Butternut Squash and Kale Salad

Serves: 4-6

Cooking time: 30-40 minutes

Ingredients:

<u>For salad:</u>

- 1 large butternut squash, deseeded, peeled, cut into small cubes

- 4 cups chopped kale (discard hard stems or ribs)

- 8 cups spinach

- 1 cup cranberries, dried

- 1/2 cup crumbled feta cheese

- 1/2 cup walnuts, chopped

- Salt and pepper, to taste

- Extra-virgin olive oil, to drizzle

<u>For dressing:</u>

- 4 tablespoons white wine vinegar

- 1/2 cup apple cider vinegar

- 2 tablespoons brown mustard

- Salt to taste

- 1/4 teaspoon pepper or to taste

- 1/2 cup canna-extra-virgin olive oil

- 2 tablespoons honey

- Juice of 2 oranges

- Zest of 2 oranges, grated

- 1/2 teaspoon fresh rosemary

Method:

1. Preheat oven to 400°F.

2. Grease a baking sheet with some oil. Spread the butternut squash over it.

3. Season with salt and pepper. Drizzle oil over it.

4. Bake at 400°F for about 30-40 minutes or until cooked through and golden brown. Do not overcook. Stir a couple of times while baking.

5. Set aside the butternut squash to cool.

6. Meanwhile, make the dressing as follows: Add all the ingredients for dressing except oil into a blender. Blend until smooth. With the blender running, drizzle canna-oil in a thin stream through the feeder tube of the blender. Blend on low until the mixture is emulsified.

7. Pour dressing over the salad. Toss well and serve.

Cranberry Walnut Salad

Serves: 2

Cooking Time: NA

Ingredients:

For salad:

- 4 cups baby spinach

- 3 tablespoons crumbled feta cheese

- 1/4 cup crushed walnuts

- 1 Fuji apple, cored, thinly sliced

- 3 tablespoons dried cranberries

For apple cider cannabis vinaigrette:

- 2 tablespoons canna-extra-virgin olive oil

- 1/4 teaspoon Dijon mustard

- 1/8 teaspoon garlic powder

- 1/8 teaspoon dried basil

- 1/8 teaspoon dried oregano

- Salt to taste

- Freshly ground pepper to taste

- 2 tablespoons apple cider vinegar

- 1/2 teaspoon light brown sugar

- 1/4 teaspoon pepper or to taste

Method:

1. Make the dressing as follows: Add all the ingredients for dressing except oil into a blender. Blend until smooth. With the blender running, drizzle canna-oil in a thin stream through the feeder tube of the blender. Blend on low until the mixture is emulsified.

2. Transfer to a bowl. Cover and set aside for a while to allow the flavors to mingle.

3. Add all the ingredients for salad into a bowl and toss well.

4. Pour dressing on top of salad. Toss well and serve.

Kale Salad with Cannabutter Vinaigrette

Serves: 2

Cooking time: 10 minutes

Ingredients:

<u>For the salad:</u>

- 1/2 pound Tuscan kale, torn or chopped into bite-size pieces (discard hard ribs and stems)

- 1/4 cup almonds, slivered and toasted

<u>For vinaigrette:</u>

- 3 tablespoons cannabutter

- 3 tablespoons unsalted butter

- Salt to taste

- 3 tablespoons sherry vinegar or red wine vinegar

Method:

1. For brown butter vinaigrette: Place a small pan over high heat. Add unsalted butter and cook until brown.

2. Stir in cannabutter. When it melts, turn off the heat.

3. Stir in the vinegar and salt to taste.

4. Place kale in a bowl. Sprinkle almonds on top. Pour vinegar over it. Toss well and serve.

Cannabis-Infused Greek Salad

Serves: 2-3

Cooking time: 12-15 minutes

Ingredients:

<u>For salad:</u>

- 1/2 tablespoon extra-virgin olive oil
- 1/2 teaspoon fresh oregano, finely chopped
- 1 chicken breast, boneless
- 1/2 red onion, thinly sliced
- 1/2 green pepper, chopped
- 1 small tomato, chopped
- 1/2 cucumber, sliced
- 1/2 head romaine lettuce
- 3 ounces canned black olives, pitted
- 1/2 cup crumbled feta cheese
- Salt to taste
- Pepper to taste

<u>For dressing:</u>

- 1 tablespoon red wine vinegar
- 2 tablespoons extra-virgin olive oil

- 2 teaspoons lemon juice

- 4-5 drops cannabis tincture

Method:

1. Place a skillet over medium-high heat. Add oil and heat. Add chicken and cook until the underside is golden brown. Flip sides and cook until golden brown on both sides.

2. Remove chicken from the pan and place on cutting board. When cool enough to handle, cut into slices.

3. Meanwhile, add all the ingredients for dressing into a small jar. Fasten the lid. Shake the jar vigorously until well combined.

4. Add lettuce, olives, red onion, cucumber, green pepper, and tomato into a bowl and toss well.

5. Drizzle the dressing on top. Toss well.

6. Divide into plates. Place chicken on top. Sprinkle oregano and feta cheese on top and serve.

CHAPTER FIFTEEN

Pineapple Express Upside-Down Cake

Serves: 4-5

Cooking time: 45 minutes

Ingredients:

- 3-4 canned pineapple slices, drained

- 1/4 cup + 1 tablespoon firmly packed light brown sugar

- 1 cup granulated sugar

- 6 tablespoons cannabutter, at room temperature

- 1 cup cake flour

- 1/2 teaspoon salt

- 3/4 tablespoon dark rum

- 1 egg

- 6 tablespoons milk

- 3/4 teaspoon vanilla extract

- 1/2 teaspoon + 1 pinch baking powder

- 3-4 maraschino cherries

Method:

1. Preheat oven to 350°F.

2. Place rack in the lower third position in the oven.

3. Grease a small round pie pan of about 6-7 inches diameter with some oil or butter.

4. Place pineapple slices on the bottom of the pan. Arrange them so they're not overlapping.

5. Add 3 tablespoons cannabutter, 1/4 cup light brown sugar, and 1/4 cup granulated sugar into a saucepan.

6. Place the saucepan over medium heat. When butter melts, turn off the heat and stir until sugar is dissolved completely.

7. Pour this mixture all over the pineapple slices in the pan.

8. Sift cake flour, baking powder, and salt in a bowl.

9. Add rum, milk, 1 tablespoon brown sugar, and vanilla into a bowl and whisk well.

10. Beat together 3 tablespoons cannabutter and remaining sugar with an electric mixer until fluffy. Add egg and beat well. Add vanilla extract.

11. Set the mixer on low and add flour and milk, a little at a time, and beat until just combined (only fold and do not overbeat).

12. Pour into the dish, over the pineapple slices.

13. Bake at 350°F for about 35-40 minutes or until done.

14. Turn off the oven and let the dish remain in the oven for 10 minutes.

15. Remove from the oven and let cool for 12-15 minutes. Loosen the edges and invert on a plate.

16. Cut into 4-5 slices. Place a cherry in the center of each slice and serve.

Banana Marijuana Ice Cream

Serves: 12

Cooking time: 5 minutes

Ingredients:

- 1/2 stick butter

- 10 tablespoons sugar

- 1/8 teaspoon salt

- 6 tablespoons rum

- 0.7 ounces finely ground marijuana

- 36 ounces cream

- 30 ounces bananas, peeled

- 10 tablespoons honey

Method:

1. Add cream to a saucepan. Place saucepan over medium heat. When the cream is well heated but not boiling, stir in the marijuana. Mix well and turn off the heat.

2. Add butter, sugar, and salt to another saucepan. Place over low heat. When butter melts, turn off the heat and stir until well combined.

3. Add the cream mixture into the butter saucepan and whisk well.

4. Mash the bananas in a bowl. Pour in the cream mixture and mix well.

5. Add honey and rum and beat until well combined.

6. Transfer into a freezer-safe container. Cover with a lid and freeze. After 3 hours, remove the ice cream from the freezer and transfer the ice cream into a chilled bowl.

7. Whisk well. Cover with cling film and freeze until firm. 30 minutes before serving, remove the ice cream from the freezer and place in the refrigerator.

8. Scoop and serve.

Dank Cheesecake

Serves: 8

Cooking time: 60 minutes

Ingredients:

- 2/3 cup cannabutter, softened

- 4 packages (8 ounces each) cream cheese, softened, at room temperature

- 2/3 cup milk

- 1 cup sour cream

- 4 tablespoons all-purpose flour

- 2 premade graham cracker crusts (9 ounces each)

- 1 1/2 cups white sugar

- 4 eggs

- 3 teaspoons vanilla extract

Method:

1. Preheat oven to 350°F.

2. Add cannabutter, cream cheese, and sugar to a mixing bowl. Beat until smooth and frothy.

3. Beat in the milk, vanilla, sour cream, eggs, and flour.

4. Divide and pour into the crusts.

5. Bake at 350°F for about 1 hour.

6. Let sit for 5 hours inside the oven.

7. Chill for about 2-3 hours.

8. Slice and serve.

Marijuana Chocolate Chip Cookies

Serves: 20-30

Cooking time: 10-12 minutes

Ingredients:

- 5 cups flour

- 2 teaspoons salt

- 2 ounces butter

- 12 ounces cannabutter

- 2 teaspoons baking soda

- 2 big cups brown sugar (do not pack)

- 1 1/2 cups sugar

- 4 eggs

- 2 teaspoons vanilla extract

- 3 1/2 cups chocolate chips

Method:

1. Preheat oven to 375°F.

2. Add flour, baking soda, and salt to a bowl and mix until well combined.

3. Beat together cannabutter, brown sugar, and sugar with an electric beater on high until fluffy. Add vanilla extract. Beat well.

4. Add the eggs, one at a time and beat well each time.

5. Add flour and mix well.

6. Add chocolate chips and mix well.

7. Scoop out cookies and place on a lined baking sheet. Leave a gap between the cookies (about an inch).

8. Bake at 375°F for 10-12 minutes.

9. Remove the baking sheet from the oven. Loosen the cookies with a metal spatula after 5 minutes

10. Cool well.

11. Serve or store in an airtight container.

Cannabis Caramels

Serves: 35-40

Cooking time: 15 minutes

Ingredients:

- 2 cups cannabutter

- 1/4 teaspoon salt

- 2 cans (14 ounces each) sweetened condensed milk

- 4 1/2 cups brown sugar

- 2 cups light corn syrup

- 2 teaspoons vanilla extract

Method:

1. Add butter, salt, and brown sugar to a pan. Place pan over medium heat. Mix well.

2. Add light corn syrup and stir. Cook for 3-4 minutes.

3. Stir in the milk. Cook until the candy feels like a firm ball when you touch it.

4. Turn off the heat. Add vanilla and stir.

5. Transfer to a rectangular pan. Cool completely. Cut into pieces. Wrap and store.

Pumpkin Cheesecake Smoothie

Serves: 4

Cooking Time: NA

Ingredients:

- 4 cups vanilla almond milk
- 4 tablespoons Ancient Delight Superfood Mix*
- 1/2 teaspoon pure almond extract
- 1/2 teaspoon pure vanilla extract
- 4 tablespoons canned pumpkin
- 2 heaping tablespoons canna-coconut oil
- 2 bananas, sliced, frozen
- 1/4 cup raw cashews
- 4 tablespoons cream cheese

Optional toppings:

- Ground cinnamon
- 4 cinnamon sticks
- Crushed graham crackers

Method:

1. *If you do not have Ancient Delight Superfood Mix, mix together 1/2 teaspoon ground nutmeg, 1 teaspoon ground cinnamon, 2 tablespoons chia seeds, and 1/2 teaspoon ground ginger in a bowl.

2. Add the smoothie ingredients to the blender and blend until smooth.

3. Pour into glasses. Top with optional toppings and serve.

Marbled Marijuana Brownie Bars

Serves: 6-8

Cooking time: minutes

Ingredients:

- 1 package (8 ounces) cream cheese, softened

- 1 tablespoon granulated sugar

- 1/2 package (from a 21 ounce package) brownie mix. Make the batter following the instructions on the package, but use canna-oil or cannabutter instead of oil or butter

- 1 egg

- 1/2 teaspoon vanilla extract

Method:

1. Preheat oven to 350°F.

2. Add cannabutter, cream cheese, eggs, vanilla, and sugar to a mixing bowl. Beat with an electric mixer until smooth and creamy.

3. Grease a small baking dish with cooking spray. Spread half the prepared brownie batter in the dish.

4. Spread cream cheese mix over the batter. Spread remaining batter over the cream cheese layer.

5. Bake at 350°F for 30-40 minutes.

6. Take out of the oven and cool completely.

7. Cut into bars and serve.

No-Bake Almond-Butter Canna-Cookies

Serves: 12-15

Cooking time: 5 minutes

Ingredients:

- 2 tablespoons unrefined canna-coconut oil

- 6 tablespoons unrefined coconut oil

- 1/2 cup grade B maple syrup or honey

- 1 cup creamy almond butter

- 1/4 teaspoon sea salt

- 3/4 cup cocoa powder

- 2 cups thick rolled oats

- Sea flakes, to top

- A handful almonds, chopped, to top

Method:

1. Place a sheet of parchment paper over a large baking sheet.

2. Add coconut oil and canna-coconut oil into a saucepan. Place saucepan over medium heat. When the oils melt, add cocoa powder, maple syrup, and almond butter. Mix until well combined. Turn off the heat.

3. Add rolled oats and salt and mix well.

4. Scoop the mixture onto the baking sheet. Flatten slightly.

5. Top with sea salt flakes and almonds.

6. Chill until firm.

7. Serve. Leftovers can be stored in an airtight container. Place in the refrigerator until ready to use.

Cannabis Peanut Butter Fudge

Serves: 18-20

Cooking time: 2-4 minutes + 1 hour cooling

Ingredients:

- 2 cups unsalted cannabutter

- 2 cups smooth natural peanut butter

- 2 teaspoon vanilla extract

- 1/2 teaspoon salt

- 2 pounds powdered sugar

Method:

1. Add cannabutter, peanut butter, and salt to a microwave safe dish. Microwave on high for 2 minutes or until completely melted. Stir a couple of times while melting.

2. Add vanilla and sugar powder. Mix well.

3. Line a baking pan with parchment paper.

4. Spread the peanut butter mixture into the pan. Spread evenly with an offset spatula.

5. Cover the pan with plastic wrap. Chill for about an hour.

6. Cut into 1-inch squares.

7. Can last for a week in the refrigerator.

Piña Co-Canna Pie Cake

Serves: 10

Cooking Time: NA

Ingredients:

- 3/4 cup graham crumbs

- 1 package (8 ounces) cream cheese, softened

- 1/4 cup Cool Whip

- 1/4 cup cherries, diced

- 1/4 cup cannabutter, softened

- 1/4 cup cream of coconut

- 1/4 cup pineapple, crushed, diced

- 1/2 cup shredded coconut

Method:

1. Add cannabutter and graham crackers to a bowl and stir well.

2. Take a small baking pan and place the cracker crumb mixture in it. Spread evenly onto the bottom of the pan. Press well.

3. Add cream cheese and cream of coconut into a bowl and beat until creamy.

4. Fold in the Cool Whip, cherries, and pineapple.

5. Spoon the mixture on the cracker crust.

6. Sprinkle shredded coconut on top.

7. Place the pie cake in the refrigerator for 2-3 hours.

8. Slice and serve.

Raspberry Peach Cannabis Cobbler

Serves: 3-4

Cooking time: minutes

Ingredients:

<u>For cobbler:</u>

- 1 cup sliced fresh peach, peeled, pitted

- 1 1/2 cups fresh raspberries

- 3 tablespoons sugar

- 1 tablespoon lemon juice or to taste

- 1/2 tablespoon all-purpose flour

- Pinch ground cinnamon

<u>For cobbler topping:</u>

- 2 tablespoons cannabutter, melted

- 3 tablespoons packed brown sugar

- 1/4 teaspoon crushed pecans or almonds

- Large pinch ground cinnamon

- 1/3 cup rolled oats

- 1/2 teaspoon pure vanilla extract

- 1/8 teaspoon salt

- 3 tablespoons all-purpose flour

Method:

1. Preheat oven to 350°F.

2. To make filling: Add peach to a bowl. Sprinkle sugar, flour, cinnamon, and lemon over it. Mix well.

3. Add raspberries and stir until well combined. Do not overmix.

4. Transfer to a greased baking dish. Spread evenly.

5. To make cobbler topping: Add brown sugar, flour, oats, vanilla, cinnamon, pecans, and salt to a bowl and mix well.

6. Add melted cannabutter and mix well.

7. Spread this mixture over the fruit filling.

8. Bake at 350°F for 30-40 minutes.

9. Remove from the oven and cool for a few minutes.

10. Serve warm with vanilla ice cream if desired.

Pot Pastelitos

Serves: 18

Cooking time: 30 minutes

Ingredients:

- 2 premade sheets of puff pastry dough

- Fruit filling of your choice

- Canna-honey, as required

- Simple syrup to serve

Method:

1. Preheat oven to 350°F.

2. Place the puff pastry sheets on your countertop.

3. Cut each of the sheets into 9 equal squares.

4. Place a teaspoon of the fruit filling in the middle of each square. Drop 3-4 drops of canna-honey over it.

5. Bring 2 opposite corners together and press them together so you have puff pastry triangles with fruit filling in the center.

6. Press the corners with fork.

7. Place the triangles on a baking sheet. Brush simple syrup over the triangles.

8. Bake at 350°F for 20 to 30 minutes.

9. Remove from the oven and cool.

10. Serve warm or cold.

11. Leftovers can be stored in an airtight container.

CONCLUSION

I want to thank you once again for purchasing this book. I hope it proved to be an enjoyable and informative read.

In this book, you were given all the information that you need so that you can start cooking with cannabis. Apart from this, you were also given all the information that you will need to fully understand the benefits that cannabis offers, along with the associated risks. Armed with the information given in this book, you will be able to decide about the different things you must remember while cooking with cannabis. Regardless of whether you are thinking about cooking with cannabis or are already cooking with cannabis, there are certain mistakes that a lot of people make. By following the simple steps and tips given in this book, you can avoid those mistakes and start cooking with cannabis like a pro!

The recipes for cannabis edibles given in this book are quite easy to understand and simple to follow. Well, cooking with cannabis isn't that complicated, is it? All that you need to do is gather the right ingredients and follow the recipes given in this book. Make sure that you are cautious while cooking with cannabis. Also, it is always a good idea to consult a medical practitioner before you start consuming any cannabis-infused products. Another thing that you cannot afford to ignore is verifying whether using cannabis is legal in your area or not!

Thank you, and all the best!

Made in the USA
San Bernardino, CA
31 August 2019